THE PUNCH BOOK OF
TRAVEL

The Punch Book of Travel, containing articles
and cartoons contributed to *Punch* over the
past 100 years, is just the thing to while away
those long hours of travel on trains and boats
and planes. It should also prove useful: if you
open the book at the centre pages, and place
it over your face, it is personally guaranteed
by the editor to keep flies at bay.

The Punch Book of Travel

Edited by
William Davis

CORONET BOOKS
Hodder and Stoughton

**Also edited by William Davis,
and available in Coronet Books:**

THE PUNCH GUIDE TO GOOD LIVING
THE PUNCH BOOK OF HEALTH

Copyright © 1974 Punch Publications Limited

First published by Punch Publications Limited

Coronet edition 1975
Third impression 1979

Printed and bound in Great Britain for
Hodder and Stoughton Paperbacks, a
division of Hodder and Stoughton Ltd.,
Mill Road, Dunton Green, Sevenoaks,
Kent (Editorial Office: 47 Bedford
Square, London, WC1 3DP) by
Hazell Watson & Viney Ltd.,
Aylesbury, Bucks

ISBN 0 340 20275 0

CONTENTS

INTRODUCTION

NOT long ago a travel firm announced, with regret, that it was cancelling its "escapist hideouts" programme because it was attracting too many customers. The boom in escapism has certainly produced novel schemes—archaeological digs, adventure trekking expeditions, Yoga holidays, dull but allegedly uplifting weeks in remote monasteries. A popular feature of the annual Brighton Festival is a conducted tour of the town's sewers, which you may feel takes the whole escapist business just a shade too far. Then there is that other phenomenon, the business study tour. Organ connoisseurs take themselves off to Germany, railway enthusiasts' rush to Portugal, and Jersey market gardeners fly to Israel to study the packing of tomatoes. British Airways has a "library" of tours for dentists, bankers, hoteliers, lawyers, and just about every other profession you can think of. The Australian Tourist Commission publishes a fat volume of costed itineries for beekeepers, cattlemen, fruit-growers, horse-breeders, Jersey cattle-breeders, wool-growers, timber operators—yes, and even investors. The Swiss are well organised too. Don't think their specialist tours are confined to horse safaries in the the Jura, mule safaris in the Valais and yoga in the Alps. Most Swiss tours seem to take in a visit to Grueres, to watch how they put holes in the cheese. The potential, clearly, is endless—an undertakers' tour of European graveyards, a cushion-stuffers trip to Nepal, a comedians' tour of American Women's Clubs. One enterprising London company has, for some years now, run a Jack the Ripper tour. Take it from there.

Meanwhile, though, there is the Punch Book of Travel. It is, you will agree, a natural successor to our earlier publications in this series—the Bedside Book (which dealt mainly with the pleasure of bed), the Punch Guide to Good Living, and the Punch Book of Women. I have, as usual, included contributions from the past as well as the present so that you can make your own comparison. Some people sigh for the days when it took a week to get from London to Brighton. Not me: I love speed. Give me a comfortable seat on a jumbo jet and I am happy. I don't feel romantic about ships, and trains bore me. I suppose I shall feel different in twenty years time, but right now flying holds immense appeal. And I appreciate my comforts, which is one reason why I distrust that over-used word "unspoiled". It often means that there is no electricity, little water, lots of mosquitoes, undrinkable wine, boring food, primitive ablutions, and camp beds as hard as rock. I can do without television and newspapers, but I can't do without soft beds, clean sheets, showers, good food, cold beer and the occasional bottle of champagne. At least I don't see why I should. These are the things I like to come back to after an active day on the sea, or a long walk in the hills.

Some forms of travel, of course, can be both tiring and tiresome. There is nothing glamorous, for example, in making your fourteenth trip to Frankfurt or Brussels. (Not that anyone at home will ever believe you). But I am willing to take my chances, and so are most of the well-travelled contributors to this book. See you in New York, Paris or Bonn.   William Davis.

On Her Majesty's Travel Service

by appointment, BASIL BOOTHROYD

"GREENLAND?" I said. "What on earth am I supposed to wear in Greenland?"

It was going to be early February when my—well, I say my—Andover of the Queen's Flight put down on the rim of the ice-cap, with about thirty degrees of frost, if my information was reliable. As an ordinary traveller you worry about clothes, especially when you're due in Florida two days later, and Mexico the day after. The pores could be opening and shutting like Venetian blinds.

My palace informant raised his eye-brows, or they may just have raised themselves, on a reflex of astonishment. Silly question.

"But," he said, as soon as he'd come to terms with my inane misconception, "you'll always walk straight out of the aircraft into a heated car." So it proved. Except that in Florida it was a cooled car. The point was that it was there. Someone recently asked Queen Frederica of Greece, exiled in Rome, what she most missed. It gave her pause. "I think," she finally said, "coming out of a building and not finding a car waiting."

Undoubtedly an honest answer. Lord Chamberlains are dispensable, also detectives keeping vigil outside the bedroom, but to find no chauffeur standing to attention with a glove on the door handle is a shaker. Particularly today, when getting from one place to another is the real killer, whether it's Epping to Liverpool Street or London to Sydney. If there's any fun to be had from hanging around airports straining for the announcements that your 747 is delayed an hour and a half . . . three hours . . . won't be flying at all, Royalty gets done out of it. When the programme says that the aircraft will depart at 0900, that's what happens, with boring inevitability. Nor are the letters ETA to be seen in those programmes. Times of arrival that are merely estimated are for you and me. (That Florida touchdown was programmed for 1610. "Prince Philip flies in on the dot," said the next day's paper.)

It isn't mere pernicketiness. Royal timetables are finely calculated, and locked on to elaborate preparations at the other end. So it's partly good manners. The Queen might be a little put out, even on her own account, to arrive behind schedule at Vancouver, Buenos Aires or Haywards Heath, and Prince Philip a little more so, the Navy efficiency streak still being strong; but they'd both be more upset at upsetting their hosts. And it's partly practical. Start even ten minutes late on one of those crammed programmes and it means a domino effect through the whole day (with rare breathing-spaces the first to go). All that aside, there's the image to think of. When the plane puts down, the car rolls into view, the Yacht warps in, on the designated minute, the waiting crowd, though they expected nothing different, thrill to the actuality all the same.

As to the clothes for Greenland, or indeed anywhere, they just don't come into it. They're there when you get there. The agonies of packing, from the frenzied sponge-bag to a suitable climatic selection and the right ribbons on the right uniforms, are taken care of by others. There is no personal humping. ("1630: The Travelling Yeoman departs with the heavy luggage from the Privy Purse Quadrangle door . . .") And no anxieties about whether your tail coat or favourite ball-gown is strangling to death in transit, because it hangs with everything else, secure from crush, in one of the aircraft's wardrobes. Royalty, as you may have noticed and taken for granted, emerges at journey's end with its creases in the right places and nowhere else, an enviable contrast with the bundles of exhausted and crumpled rubbish seen in the airports of the world dragging their scuffed shoes in the direction of Baggage Reclaim.

All Royal aircraft are subject to what RAF Benson calls re-roling, a word that comes off less frighteningly in print than it does on the nervous ear. It means that the insides can be torn out and reconstituted to suit the length of the trip and the size of the party. In the Andovers it happens on a lesser scale. They aren't in any case big enough for the full retinue taken on big, slap-up visits overseas, are strictly only short-haul aircraft (and turbo-prop, not full jet),

"Even if it does work, who'd want to arrive anywhere looking like that?"

and only take the punishment they do because of intensive maintenance. The engines are changed while still in their prime, and the wealth of spares would practically build a fresh aeroplane.* But a Super VC 10, say, hired from BOAC—and serviced, no doubt, with equal care—can change its internal arrangements even between flying out and flying back. Conference rooms, divans, bars, dressing-rooms can come and go, multiply or diminish.

Of the Royal Train I know nothing, except that it's used less often than you'd expect. "Overnight Train to Scotland," when it appears on the engagement card, usually means an ordinary sleeper. Given fair weather, *Britannia* is plainly the most desirable way of getting from A to B; not to say the most prestigious, a small, immaculate bit of Britain, swanning impressively around the world. I was only in her once. The routine emergency instructions in my cabin gave my boat station as "Royal Barge." Before lunch the next day I found myself automatically touching one of the many arrangements of silver-vased pink roses. Well, these days you can't tell, can you? The plastic flowers are so clever . . . Again the hardships of travel are agreeably minimised. No need for any oneupmanship to get a decent table in the dining saloon or a chair in the sun that hasn't been illicitly, yet somehow unarguably, pre-empted by an unscrupulous towel; none of those hellish queues to press complaints on the harassed purser, and no swindles by the indigenous cab-drivers at ports of call (a Rolls has been swayed aboard, and gleams darkly in its purpose-built deck housing).

On the other hand, you and I haven't got to shake a thousand hands, remember a thousand names, be continuously bright at banquets. If the prospect of the Captain's cocktail party weighs heavy on us, we can always cut it. If we want to go ashore alone and sit awhile on a warm bollard, that's all right. In *Britannia*, except for actual sea time—and even then the office work goes on, and the red dispatch boxes come and go—there's no cutting anything.

Those who have been in the Royal service, and quit, come down to earth with a painful thud. They've travelled in style, by land, air and water, and forgotten the irritations and indignities of cancelled trains and unobtainable cabs, airport din and confusion and delays, the privations of the cruise ship's guided tour round the beauty spots (including those late starts and unappetising mass lunches), and after one or two ventures into the world of travel as most of us know it, they decide to stay at home.

I only had the merest sniff of it, myself. But it's surprising how quickly you get used to it. After twenty-five years or so I can understand the Duke's darkened brow on the rare occasions when he walks out of the aircraft and finds nothing but tarmac.

It happened to me at Mexico City, after less than a week of the top travel treatment. I'd been whirled off as to the manner born at Stornoway, Keflavik, Sondrestrom, Goose Bay, Ottawa, Merida; but at Mexico City, as programmed, the Royal party whirled off and left me. It's a shock, just when you've developed a taste for the golden life, finding yourself alone, six thousand feet up, and nothing for comfort but a distant view of snow-capped Popocatepetl.

NO, BUT I READ THE BROCHURE

in which ALAN COREN fails even to travel hopefully.

IT is not every day of the week—fortunately—that mankind, groping its way through this vale of tears in the desperate hope that somewhere along the route there may be a small patch of smile and a watery sun falling on a dropped half-crown, gets hit in the face with a brick. Our disappointments and disillusions tend to accrete slowly as we grope; gradual, almost imperceptible, wanings of expectation, accompanied (such is the grace of God) by the shrugged acceptance that comes of long lousy experience. Thunderbolts are few.

Last week, however, a chunk of firmament came belting through the upper air and buried itself in the sod beneath, leaving a crater that we shall henceforth be unable to ignore. Poor sod! I hear you cry, and right you are. The missile in question, which may well be known from now on as Mynett's Comet, was a chunk of jagged and unalloyed truth, no less terrible for the fact that it came as poetry. I quote:

"It is very rare that the sea and the sky are as blue as they are made out to be, that the flowers are so brilliant, and the women so beautiful."

Now, you could be forgiven for thinking that this impeccable trope was the work of a major poet, about to snuff it upon his garret mattress and wishing to leave a moving *mot* behind, the bequest of his sensitivity to us still-seeking survivors. But no: that sentence was not delivered among guttering candles, with elderly mistresses blowing their conks on the eiderdown and the dog moaning in the grate; it zonked to an astonished world in the prose-panelled environs of the High Court, and it fell out of a space just below the austere wig of Judge Mynett, in the course of his finding for the defendants Global Tours Ltd. And though it will change the lives of all of us, it was primarily directed at the plaintiff, Mr. Ronald Lee, late of Melbourne, Australia.

Because Mr. Lee had claimed damages against Global on the grounds that their tour, for which he had forked out the proceeds from the sale of his Melbourne house, had not lived up to the promise of its brochure. Among other things, complained Mr. Lee, the Tower of Pisa didn't lean half as much as he'd been led to believe it would.

Now, many of us, I'm sure, will sympathise with Mr. Lee's disappointment: it's no joke coming thirteen thousand miles to the Tower of Pisa, only to find you can walk under it without taking your hat off. My wife and I once made a journey as lengthy as Mr. Lee's, and rather, I would guess, more arduous, involving as it did not merely aircraft and trains, but also Landrovers, pack mules, and boots, in temperatures that started in the high hundreds and subsequently dropped to the low tens, to see the highest mountain in the world. Upon arrival at the vantage-point, the Nepalese guide cried dramatically: "There! Mount Everest!" and my wife said: "Where?" and the guide pointed furiously at a rather low lump indistinguishable from the rather more impressive cloud that hung round it and screamed: "There!" and my wife said: "It's not even pointed," and that was that.

It was on the same trip, incidentally, that we trudged to see the Taj Mahal by moonlight, and as we came round the corner the moon went in, and we couldn't even see the guide.

It is at this juncture that I find it necessary to draw a distinction between me (and, I imagine, the vast majority of you) and two other blokes: Mr. Lee, on the one hand, and Judge Mynett, on the other. We are different from Mr. Lee in that we *accept* these sorts of disappointment; we are prepared to live with the fact that a tall citizen has interposed himself between us and the Changing of the Guard, that Anne Hathaway's cottage has the decorators in, that there is nothing about the Sphinx that is inscrutable, it is merely that it is chipped on the lip; and we do not hale the heirs and assigns of William Wordsworth before the magistrate simply because earth actually does have things to show more fair than the view from Westminster Bridge and the Shell Building doesn't seem to be asleep. And we are different from Judge Mynett in that we would never in a million years accept that all promise is doomed to unfulfilment, all expectation headed for disappointment, all rainbows sure to end in a crock of brass. If every party we have ever attended was full of pallid flat-chested women talking to witless boorish men, and hosted by a man whose vinophilia stops at Libyan advokaat and a woman unable to defrost a pea without assistance, shall we therefore accept

"Yes, but on the credit side the smell's completely disappeared."

*" You English! 'Ow can we finish the hotel on time when
we have to pick you up from the airport?"*

no invitations? Rubbish! Somewhere, under the stars, the beautiful
people are throwing the binge to end them all, and next time,
perhaps . . .

Likewise, holidays. Simply because the jewel of the Adriatic
turned out to be a line of chip shops, and the golden sands of Tunisia
have yet to be cleared of Rommel's mines, and the view from our
balcony towards Capri was somewhat flawed by the crane in between, should we despair, Your Honour, of ever finding Paradise
at 69gns for fifteen days, including beach cabana and half-bott.
wine with evening meal?

The point to which I would direct the Court is that while its
judgement may very well be true, it is not a truth with which we
care to be presented. You shouldn't go around saying those kind of
things, Judge. People will start believing you. And the joy of annual
brochuring, so infinitely more pleasurable than the joy of annual
holidaying, would be dead.

I think it already is, for me. The Court, as courts will from time
to time, has established a precedent. I have before me a brochure,
from which I have so far spent many happy hours picking likely
spots for this summer's brief escape, juggling them, matching one
against another, trying to judge whether the sea is greener in Corsica
than in Rhodes, the sky bluer in Nice than in Agadir, the busts larger
in Portugal than in Greece. In the Hotel Saronga Playa, it is not
possible to fight one's way to the bar for the unaccompanied bikinis
thronging the lino; the Hotel Coral Playa, I see, has a totally empty
swimming-pool that dwarfs the Mediterranean beyond it; at a
restaurant in sunsoaked (yet breeze-softened) Corfu, a nude seems
to be eating a lobster, or possibly vice-versa, while in the bedroom
of the hotel above, the bed sports a length of sun-ripened nubilia
that would make a bishop kick a hole in a stained-glass window.
The lounge of the Hotel La Romantica seem built to accommodate

not merely the Concorde but also the requisite runway, and a regiment of waiters can actually be seen *running*. I cannot swear, but I believe there are nuts in the dishes; certainly, the premises are rife with the sort of cleavage rarely seen this side of Raquel Welch. Or that side, either.

That the ten Miss World finalists standing on the beach at Hammamet, holding a beach ball and apparently looking for a goalie, will still be there after I've unpacked, I am in no position to swear. But—and here, Your Honour, is the bitter nub—nor am I any longer in a position even to dream about. As I stare at them now, I hear your dread words ringing about me, and the varicose veins begin to creep along their legs, and their superstructures begin to sag, and, one by one, their spotless teeth fall out. I look at the hotel behind them, and I can see the artist's cunning, brushing in the roof they haven't built yet, brushing out the gas-station that separates it from the sea; and, peering closer, I know that the photographer's wide-angle lens has created a Beverley Hills seraglio out of a boot-cupboard where you can't get into bed without putting the wardrobe on the balcony and the only way you can take a shower is to stand on the lidless lavatory and bang the ceiling until the condensation falls on you. And that when I get down to dinner at last, the lift having conked out the day before, everything will be off; which will subsequently turn out to be the only stroke of luck I have for the entire fortnight.

Ah, well, leave us be mature about all this, it was bound to come; as Judge Mynett (and where the hell does *he* go when he feels like a paddle and a pistachio cone?) pointed out in his shattering summing-up: "No-one but a child takes glossy brochures seriously." I always knew that childhood had something going for it, but I could never quite put my finger on what it was, till now.

"I've won ten days in Paris with the companion of my choice."

Kitting Out and Dashing Off

by ffolkes

"*I think perhaps a little more padding in the shoulders.*"

"*No, madam, you don't actually **wear** the mosquito net.*"

"*I bet that suit could tell some stories.*"

"*I'm sorry, sir, we don't stock goggles.*"

"*I want something that will stand out on a
package flight to Honduras.*"

Damn the Expenses!

Take a tip from GEORGE MIKES and pay your own way

EXPENSE-ACCOUNT air travellers have a uniform of their own. Ordinary humans keep their green boarding cards, slightly bashfully, in their inside pockets or buried between pages of their passports; expense-account travellers always display them in their cigar pockets (I believe that is the official name of the pocket on a man's left chest). The vivid pink sticking out of the pocket broadcasts to the world: "Look at me, I'm travelling first class!" People throw envious glances at these chaps and treat them with respect. But I know better and when I see one of them I think: "Poor bastard. I do feel sorry for you. I know what you are in for."

Normally I pay for my own tickets (green card, inside pocket) but it has happened that I was sent somewhere by a paper, a broadcasting company, a national tourist office or an air line. I always find these occasions pretty harrowing.

First of all, on entering the airport building you are paged or received rather ceremoniously by a P.R.O. and led into the VIP lounge. I hate the very idea of humanity being divided into VIPs and VUPs—very important and very unimportant persons. I fail to see why the chairman of a corporation is more important than an unemployed railway porter or a bum. Richer; better off; luckier; more pompous—yes. But more important? I always have the inclination to go to the VUP lounge but there is no appeal. The VIP lunch is full of businessmen, minor diplomats—well, what if major diplomats?—and they all look like people who are carrying the burden of the world on their shoulders. They all have their pink cards sticking out of their pockets and have huge, large briefcases which they can hardly lift. They are offered drinks (at 9 a.m.) and are not in a position to refuse a double whisky or a treble brandy because that would look very un-VIP-ish. You find a telephone in front of your armchair, placed on a low table, and you are told that you might use it free of charge. It is added very politely, in a soft voice but most emphatically: "For local calls." Whom the hell can

"For heaven's sake, Edith, you're not going to send a card to the damned dog?"

"Don't tell me . . . we're to accompany Pharoah on his long journey to the sun, tourist class."

you ring at 9 a.m.? Just because the call is free. But all those other chaps, in dark suits, wearing horn-rimmed spectacles, are busy making one call after the other. They all keep their voices down and, I am convinced, they are rhubarbing away—some in English, some in Arabic or Swedish. So I ring my home and ask, grimly, whether there are any messages. As I had left my home half an hour before for three months, I cannot really expect a pile of important messages to have arrived between 8.30 and 9 a.m. So I am told: "Oh hell . . ." and I hear my good lady turning over to the other side and banging the receiver down. I nod gravely and put the receiver down myself slowly and thoughtfully as if I had heard dramatic and important news. I try to look like the man who, shattering though the problem may be, is capable of dealing with it. So the journey begins and so it goes on to the bitter end.

But I have had much worse expense account trips and they still give me nightmares. I was asked by a famous and rich American daily to write a piece on Germans holidaying at German resorts, with special attention to the changing German character. They offered me a fabulous fee and I accepted the assignment with alacrity. Then I was passed on to the Business Manager to discuss the details of my German trip. German trip?—I asked. I knew Germany, its resorts and its people inside out. I meant to sit down then and there and hand over my copy an hour later. The Business Manager said that as I knew Germany so well, perhaps a sojourn of seven weeks might be sufficient. But if I preferred ten or twelve weeks it was most certainly O.K. with them. I was absolutely horrified. Having been away in New York, I just could not spare all that time in Germany. So I said firmly:

"God, no. I don't need seven weeks. All I need really . . ." I looked at his face and I knew that my whole assignment was in the gravest danger. "All I need is three weeks."

"Four," he said firmly.

All right, four. Then he proceeded to explain about expenses. I

19

expected a stern admonishment to be thrifty. But in fact I received a stern admonishment to be madly extravagant. He made me understand—although he did not say so in so many words—that I was not to ruin the market for others. I would be regarded as a traitor, a black-leg and would never be used again. I was expected to spend £35 a day as a minimum as everyone else did. As he did not trust me and was horrified that I might try to save money for them, he gave me some broad hints.

"You will have to entertain people for lunch *and* dinner every day. Breakfast is also a wonderful time for discussions—but you must offer really sumptuous breakfasts if you call out people so early. You will use a lot of taxis and may hire cars. You offer people drinks. You may have to arrange parties. Often for twenty people. Sometimes for thirty." He looked deeply in my eye, he expected the message to sink in. "Thirty or more," he said emphatically. "You will need to buy a lot of books and periodicals. Keep all the receipts, that's vitally important. Hotel bills, et cetera. But do not worry, as long as you have the receipts, all expenses are all right."

He gave me a large sum then and there and told me that should I need more—any amount—or should I decide to stay for eight, ten or twelve weeks, all I had to do was to ring their Frankfurt office and the money would be telegraphed to me within hours. He gave me one last, useful piece of advice.

"You will find hotel rooms claustrophobic. Not conducive for work. Always hire a suite."

He knew what he was talking about. It is not easy to spend £35 minimum a day. It is damned hard work and pretty boring, too.

Germany was full. I could not get suites and sometimes I could not get even rooms in the most expensive hotels. It was very frustrating. My friends seemed to be pleased to see me at first but avoided me like the plague soon afterwards. They could not stand the heavy meals I forced upon them. Some did not like to have steak for breakfast. I had to rely on my personal friends to be at the receiving end of my generous and aggressive hospitality. They had to come to daily parties. While they enjoyed the first, they seemed to be less enthusiastic after the eighth. Besides, they were never allowed to have a cheap German *schnapps*—their favourite—but had to drink Scotch whisky, vodka and champagne; beer—so wonderful in Germany—was out and replaced by the most expensive French vintage wines from the last century. Most of them loved to walk but those who did not possess a car were sent home by limousines hired by me. I love playing tennis but could not play on this occasion: I could not waste my time on something which did cost only a few marks per hour. As I was to write about German holiday-habits, I had to visit places where middle-aged Germans were "taking the cure". I visited the places for gout, for arthritis, for heart-cases, etc. I anticipated that gout-patients would not play tennis with me; but why were all these people so terribly dull to talk to? If they talked at all, they talked only of their gout and the eighth gout case is almost as dull as the eighth champagne-party.

At the end of the fourth week my expense-account still stood alarmingly low. I had averaged well under £35 a day. It was an American TV man I met in Bonn who solved this problem for me.

"You are a sucker. We all have this problem, there's nothing new in it. A helicopter is the answer to your prayers."

"Helicopter?"

"Yes. They go up pretty high, I mean in price."

"But what can I do in a helicopter?"

"Take photographs of German holiday-makers. They look pretty nice from a height of 5000 feet."

I hired a helicopter and circled over the town of Bochum. I took a book on ancient Aztec civilisation with me and told the pilot to go on circling around until I had finished. It took me five and a half hours to read it. The bill was not much over £100 but it helped.

Some weeks later I handed in my piece and my expense account. The accounts were all right. So was the piece but the Editor wanted a few more resorts covered and few further aspects of the German character discussed.

"You will need another three weeks in Germany for that," he declared sternly.

I turned pale.

"A few more weeks of regal luxury won't do any harm to you," the Editor added benevolently.

"I'll go to Crumlin jail in Belfast to rewrite it. To Lubyanka Prison in Moscow. I could work very well in Vorkuta Camp, Siberia. But I refuse—*refuse*—another day on expense accounts."

ON A WING AND A PRAYER

Passengers on El Al, the Israeli airline, are given a card with an appropriate prayer — Sunday Times

A General Prayer for Holidays

Keep Thou, O Lord, this Charter Flight
Safe in the bosom of the Night.
Deliver us from fret and fuss.
If not, at least deliver us.

A Prayer for Those Held Up at Airports

O Lord, waft us on the wings of the morning, or failing that the wings of the evening, or the morning after the first morning, or the evening after the first evening, even unto the seventh morning and the seventh evening. Thou knowest, Lord, we are but dross in the eyes of those that are set in authority over us, for they have tongues but speak not, and eyes that see not. Yea, and when two or three thousand are gathered together, yet are their requests not granted. But Thou, O Lord, shalt make these tyrants Thy footstool and suffer Thy servants to pass through the Departure Gates, and they shall rejoice exceedingly.

A Prayer for Those Travelling by Aeroflot, the USSR Airline

O Lord, smite not this roaring chariot, though verily it was fashioned by those who believe not in Thee, but worship strange gods and are become abominable in Thy sight. Withold, we pray thee, Thy vengeance until Thy erring servants have landed, neither punish us with cold meat balls for burnt offerings from the Galleys of Wickedness. O Lord, we have strayed into the air space of the unholy. We have left undone those things that we ought to have done; but the shafts of the seat belts are broken and Thou wilt not punish us for the sins of the Tartars and the Muscovites and all the heathen that went before them. O Lord, take us to Heathrow and we will worship Thee in Thy chapel there, though we be the first to enter its portals.

A Prayer to be Said by Returning Travellers

Lord, as we miserable sinners return from renewing our bodies in Thy life-giving Sun, give ear, we beseech Thee, to the cries and lamentations of those who dwell on the flight-path beneath, yea, even by the very House of Sion. Grant Thou, O Lord, the prime leaseholds in Thy Celestial Mansions to such as live in Richmond, Twickenham and Kew, for great have been their tribulations in this world, and let no man envy these their reward hereafter, lest he be cast into the Everlasting Bonfire.

A Prayer for Restoration of Lost Baggage and the Correction of Those Responsible

O Lord, our grips and hold-alls
    Have vanished once again.
Our bags and trunks and fold-alls
    Are lost by wicked men.

Forgive not their transgressions
    Too hastily, O Lord.
Restore us our possessions,
    Then wield Thy flaming sword.

A Prayer for Times of Turbulence

Be with us now, O Lord. And when
We're told to breathe Thy Oxygen
From dangling masks, be with us then.

Be near us, Lord. We know that flight
Is but a challenge to Thy might,
A privilege and not a right.

O Lord, whose mercy we revere,
We know we shouldn't be up here!

It was Better by Penny Farthing

E. S. TURNER re-visits the golden days of transport, when you really had to travel before you arrived.

THE transport of yesterday, by virtue of being dirty, dangerous, noisy and uncomfortable, has always enjoyed a high place in the affections of the British people.

Of course, they often had other things on their mind when travelling, and their recollections may have been coloured thereby.

A few examples:

The Char-a-Banc: "A long open vehicle with rows of transverse seats," according to the dictionary, but that fails to do justice to the glorious Passion Waggon of the 1920s. At least the dictionary gives the correct pronunciation: *shar-a-bang*. With its suggestive French name, the char-à-banc was the triumphal car of the first Age of Emancipation, filling the quiet lanes with the tumult of a Sabine Rape, bringing terror to lonely pubs and cardiac arrest to Ancient Inhabitants. In more sophisticated communities, like Southend, convoys of chars-à-banc (to use an affected plural) were welcome by cheering inhabitants as if they were the Guards Armoured Division liberating Brussels.

The char-à-banc was ideal for works outings, printers' wayzgooses, sports fans and all bodies which scorned decorum and pneumonia. On those bench seats the sexes were thrown into intimate contact, especially on bends. Sometimes a high degree of chumminess set in. Chronicles of the period tell how a lady hospital visitor at Nottingham (possibly) was surprised to find that nine women in the matern-

THE BACKFIRE

ity ward were all expecting their babies on March 1. When she said, to a tenth woman, "And I suppose yours is due on the first of March too?" the others chorused, "Oh no, she wasn't in our char-à-banc." Eventually chars-à-banc were roofed over in an effort to stop people throwing out bottles and garters, and separate seats were provided in the hope that men would keep their hands to themselves. The sight of a spanking char-à-banc in a motor museum brings tears of lascivious joy to elderly roués and their surviving trulls.

Taxi: "*Wat's the matter wiv you?*"
Hansom: "*There ain't nothing the matter wiv me.*"
Taxi: "*Then why did you give me such a nasty look?*"
Hansom: "*I didn't give it yer, you 'ad it to start wiv.*"

The Hansom Cab: An earlier Passion Waggon, strictly for two. Disraeli called it "the gondola of London," but never got the Queen into one. From its cosy interior the occupants could obtain an exciting close-up of the horse's rump. There was a little square opening in the roof through which the driver could peer to see what was going on, and if necessary charge double the fare. As a means of taking a pliant woman from one *cabinet particulier* to another, without stopping what one was doing, the hansom was invaluable. The drivers were called Jehus (II Kings ix 20) and smelled like haystacks.

The Open Aircraft: Ah, to feel the wind probing and stinging under one's helmet, gradually numbing the skull, like a deep draught of Pernod! Ah to feel the sting of the blobs of oil blown back from the engine, gradually suffusing the goggles with a blue mist! The engine always had a huge propeller, without which no aircraft is really safe, and it was flown by a "joystick," not by a computer. If the pilot turned up saying he had forgotten his maps, you gave him a

25

page torn from a school atlas and he was happy. In emergencies he didn't expect you to wing-walk but you might have to chew a lot of chewing gum to patch a leaky petrol tank; and you had to try to read the names on railway station platforms. At a pinch the pilot might ask you to throw out handfuls of mauve leaflets advertising somebody's Giant Drapery Sale, but what could be more fun? The fuselage holes were probably made by Richthofen. Jumbo jets? Faugh!

The Open Tram: All men who were men sat on the upper deck in the invigorating sleet, with their children about them, while sparks hissed down from the "fishing rod," which they occasionally helped the conductor to restore to its rail. Women sat inside, sniffing and looking at advertisements for Iron Jelloids and Owbridge's Lung Tonic. The driver had no windscreen-wiper, chiefly because he had no windscreen. Swathed in oilskins, purple-faced, he clung to the controls like the helmsman of a storm-wracked coffin ship. The decline of the tramcar dates from the decision to cover the roof and enclose the driver. From Glasgow you could travel all the way to Loch Lomond on an open tram, a journey of almost intolerable romance.

The Cyclecar: This was a collection of tubes and tie-bars mounted on three wheels, with the engine out at the front naked to the elements and ready to assimilate the shock of collisions. Ten horse-power pulling on a five-cwt. chassis—there was acceleration for you! Deceleration was another matter. The older Morgans had two independent brakes, as the law required, but each operated on the single back wheel, and if you applied both suddenly when the back wheel was in a wet tramline the results were spectacular. Easy to park—you could thrust the front into an exiguous space and then lift the rear end into position. No reverse gear, since once under way there could be no going back. The engine was started by winding a handle at the side, at the same time operating something called an exhaust valve lifter. The Morgan was driven by powerful chains, which sometimes came off and eventually stretched to nearly twice their length. Just two gears, slow and fast. Not so good on long road-up sections, for while the front wheels rode in ruts created by other cars the rear wheel bounced and slithered on the piled-up rubble between the tracks. You *could* have a snap-down hood, if you felt equal to driving at sixty miles an hour with the same amount of visibility as you could get from inside a two-slot pillar-box.

There were special magazines for cyclecar owners, who were a breed apart, had interesting scars and paid a lower road tax. But women hated three-wheelers. Buying a car with a fourth wheel was a terrible step; you felt even worse than a bicyclist turning over to a tricycle.

The Train de Luxe: (1) The Carlsbad Express. Operated by the International Sleeping Car Company, it left Victoria at ten am daily after the London Season was over, carrying people who·had overburdened their guts to the spas of Bohemia to be purged. Naturally, it fed them substantial meals all the way there and back. Really civilised living, that was. As for (2) the Orient Express, it doesn't even have a restaurant car these days. For generations all spies have gone by air. In the old days you had La Madonne des Sleepings in the berth underneath you, as indeed you did on (3) the Trans-Siberian Railway. This, of course, is still running in a pale, electrified sort of way, but you should have travelled on it in the great days of Czarist tyranny. Only £33 from Paris to Vladivostok. You had to book months ahead to be sure of a berth. At meals they served choice wines from the Imperial vineyards. They had a reading room car with a grand piano, a bath car and a chapel car. At the railside you could buy pots of caviare so that you could picnic in the buffet car between meals. There were always two ticket men—one to hold the ticket and the other to punch it. In winter they ran the rails across the ice of Lake Baikal, and what a marvellous thrill it was when the thaw came early!

The Penny Farthing: Until you've crossed the Simplon on a penny farthing, as Leonard Huxley (son of "T. H.") did, you haven't lived. On the sixty-inch high wheel you enjoyed a rolling, billowy rhythmic movement and a godlike view of the countryside, which can never be captured on one of those effete, low-slung contraptions. Don't let the Huxleys have all the fun. Steal a penny farthing now from outside your nearest folk museum and learn how to execute "headers" with aplomb.

"Sound yer 'orn!"   *"Sound your aitches!"*

"Phrase-book."

EUROPE ON $500 A DAY

ALAN WHICKER:

WHATEVER you may believe it *is* possible to Do Europe on $500 a day. Not spectacularly of course, but if you know your way round and can cut corners, tolerably well.

On so limited a budget many everyday pleasures will be beyond your purse; forget about your personal executive jet – even the modest Hawker Siddeley 125 we took to Stockholm clicked-up £225 per flying hour, plus crew expenses and landing fees; so 500 miles, a couple of smoked salmon sandwiches, and you're borrowing again.

Then there's the yacht, for that traditional milling-round-the-Med Not a wildly extravagant idea, you might think – but stuck on $500 a day, forget it. Even last year *Katy II* chartered "from" £5,000 a week, so should you and a couple of rationed friends chuck in your $500s-a-day, you'd still be pushed to get adequately afloat. Those £3,000-a-week yachts are, as you can imagine, pretty basic So who needs hard tack?

On £200 a day, keep it cool and modest; leave the bella figura to the Big Spenders.

Back in 1963 I made some television programmes about J. Paul Getty and one or two other characters who were comfortably-off. Since then, any television critics with limited resources (and some magazines not always *au courant*, like Punch) label me the Expert On Millionaires. That tired old cliché reaction was even dragged into reviews of programmes on the Stone-Age men of the New Hebrides and those adorable Poor Clares; not excatly the Monied Classes . . .

Nor, at $500 a day, are you; though in certain haunts conspicuous expenditure may still be observed: I was at Cannes with Harold Robbins, Carpetbagger Extraordinaire. Near his yacht *Gracara* (only 84 foot and, Good Lord, modest *enough*) stood a sleek and splendid mini-liner with helicopter platform on the stern. The owner, a French industrialist, passed his time on another and equally magnificent yacht anchored up the coast at St. Tropez. When he wanted a haircut his chopper would waft him the 30 miles to the branch-yacht at Cannes, where a portable bicycle was wheeled down the gangway; off he'd pedal towards the Carlton barbershop and a long-back-and-sides.

Considering cost and upkeep of two endless yachts and crews, plus helicopter and pilot, you might think it more economic to employ a personal crimper – preferably one able to hoist sails and splice mainbraces, on the side. Scrub decks, even.

But back to grim reality, and your $500 a day. You can't attain a personal jet with crew saluting and Customs cringing, but a BEA Trident will wing you to Nice, accompanied by a quarter bottle or two (are you sitting comfortably?) for a modest £57, with almost three-quarters of the day's ration still unexpired.

The South of France is not my favourite place, though Monaco retains a certain style; to move around, a classic and practical conveyance might be a 1929 Phantom II with a liveried chauffeur. A London company specialises in such gentlemanly transport; say £60 a day, plus – and still £80 worth of traveller's cheques jingling in your pocket . . . .

Trendies jeer at Monte Carlo; let them. Take a suite at the urbane Hotel de Paris (£80 a day); if you don't like the furniture, they'll change it.

On that basic allowance you'll not risk gambling, so next day move towards Cannes and the Palm Beach Casino – but only for dinner, allowing £35 a head. Watch the rich folk listlessly losing, then to the Val de Cuberte, just inland, where it's fashionable to follow King Hussein's example and swim fully clothed. This can take its toll of dinner jackets (say £130 per dive, from Doug Hayward, to measure). For the night there's Byblos at St. Trop where (like Acapulco's Las Brisas) a swimming pool comes with your suite. Ignore Carlton, Eden Roc, Martinez; infested by the resprayed white Rolls brigade of show biz and rag trade; television (groan) even.

Northwards, and Paris remains hard to ignore – especially when you realise how delightful it would be without the Parisians. Take a suite at the Plaza Athénée (£70 a day, each) or, if you're pushed, the George V (a gentle £55 a day). Shop at Cartier or Hermès, try mesclagne Mère Irma at Lasserre or noisettes d'agneau Edouard VII at Maxim's (20 a head, going easy on the wine) and on to New Jimmy's. That carefree day should show what a franc-pincher you need to be on $500 a day . . . .

Once the simplest way to ease painlessly through that daily allocation was in Jamaica, at Frenchman's Cove. For that modest sum they guaranteed anything your heart desired, from marlin fishing through Cadillacs to bathfuls of Dom Pérignon. After signing the register and, at your cottage, acknowledging butler, maid and cook, your rich little head was not worried by any request, however unreasonable: simply press the bell, and tell them. That simplified book-keeping system has gone – though not because people rang too often. Grainger Weston, then owner, told me most passing millionaires called for four-minute eggs and thin toast.

Back in Europe, staying within the limit, there's the Palace at St. Moritz, if you can stand the noise-and-the-people; my taste is more towards the Grand at Bürgenstock, above Lake Lucerne: in Springtime the air's champagne – and if nature isn't enough Sophia Loren has a pad up the road. Georges Simenon was striding about puffing his pipe when I was there – and he only lives down the hill, on the next lake.

There's the Hotel du Palais at Biarritz, once home of Empress Eugènie who wasn't exactly The Girl Next Door; but I have a nostalgia for Vienna, that so sympathetic|European|cul de sac, and the red-plush of Sacher – though how *did* that boring Torte get so famous?

The most elegant expenditure of all awaits in my favourite city: a private gondola. Price, open to negotiation – but watch it. Stay at Cipriani's, over on Giudecca, and eat simply but well at Harry's, where the crowd's worth the cash. Then drive down the leg of Italy to the Sirenuse at Positano; a moonlit dinner on that balcony is magic, at any price. Pop over to Sardinia and head north from Olbia for the Patrizza or Cala di Volpe on the Costa Smeralda; that bogus patina is by the Flintstones out of Disneyland, but still stunning. Fly on to the Madrid Ritz, where you regress an age and have to wear collar and tie to walk in the garden; but worth every peseta.

So you see if you don't spend all your daily allowance on a fine bottle of wine or one sleeve of an haute couture dress, it *is* possible to pass an agreeable time on $500 a day. Just avoid tourist traps, curb extravagance and reach for the bill *very* slowly.

At some later stage in the game we might go into 'Europe on $5,000 a day'; now *that's* a realistic budget, with possibilities . . . .

"But where's the justice? This magnificent sunset is available to any bum."

Man in Hotel by LARRY

STAND NO NONSENSE
FROM YOUR GUIDE

Are you the sort of traveller who can keep a guide in his place? This quiz will help you to decide whether you are a man or a mouse. Or a troublemaker.

1. You are on a coach trip, chatting to your companions. The guide is trying to tell you how many square miles of country-side are under beetroot. He whistles warningly into his microphone, then says, "When everybody has quite finished talking . . ." and follows it with "Perhaps somebody else would like to take over the microphone?" Would you:
    (a) Lapse into shamefaced silence;
    (b) Accept his invitation and seize the microphone;
    (c) Sit back and correct his mis-statements;
    (d) Wait till tipping time and ask him for change of five pence;
    (e) Incite your neighbours to sing "Nelly Dean".

2. Your coach guide has told you how many square miles are under beetroot and has fallen asleep. Would you:
    (a) Fall gratefully alseep too;
    (b) Waken the guide and demand more statistics, saying this is what you are paying him for;
    (c) Take over the microphone and mimic his performance;
    (d) Concentrate your charm on the divorcee from Memphis beside you.

3. Your guide has started telling a story about the Englishman, the Scotsman and the Irishman. Would you:
    (a) Interrupt him before the punch-line with a request to halt the coach at the nearest toilet;
    (b) Let him finish and threaten him with the Race Relations Board;
    (c) Stealthily disconnect the wire to the loudspeaker;
    (d) Instruct him to cut out the funny stuff and keep to the beetroot statistics.

4. Your guide is angry because the party is not marching in close formation across the Place de la Republique. Would you:

(a) Fall out and embarrass him by barking "Left, right, left . . .";

(b) Point out that some of the party are old women; like himself;

(c) Make a point of looking to the left when he draws attention to something on the right, and vice versa;

(d) Apologise and then say, "Please settle an argument: are we in Belgium or Holland?

5. Your guide has stopped the coach at what you suspect is his brother-in-law's souvenir shop. Would you:

(a) Say you have seen better stuff in a sacked Yemenite souk;

(b) Saunter ostentatiously to the establishment across the road;

(c) Stay in the coach and read the guide's *Daily Express;*

(d) Go for a walk and keep the coach waiting ten minutes.

6. The butler-guide showing you over the stately home is being very superior about the Family, as painted by Lely. Would you:

(a) Say politely, "Belt up, Jeeves";

(b) Remark that Lely was a great one for painting whores;

(c) Say you always understood the tenth earl was Jack the Ripper;

(d) Give a smart tug on the nearest bell-pull, to see what happens.

7. You are in Russia. Your Intourist guide tells you that each of the Soviet Socialist Republics is autonomous and has the right to secede from the Union at any time. Would you:

(a) Break into loud incredulous laughter;

(b) Raise a single sceptical eyebrow;

(c) Stare stonily at the nearest statue of Karl Marx;

(d) Ask him to get on with the beetroot statistics.

8. You are in America. The guide is monotonously reciting the monthly rentals of every apartment block in sight. Would you:
   (a) Ask him how much rent he pays, and how much alimony;
   (b) Insist on a proper rundown on local cultural activities;
   (c) Interrupt him and say you think someone is smoking pot;
   (d) Defect from the tour with the divorcee from Memphis;
   (e) Fit ear plugs.

9. You are in Morocco. Five hundred boys, youths and grey-beards are clamouring to be your guide. Would you:
   (a) Say something in a gibberish language, to put them off;
   (b) Hire the first ten who call you "Charlie";
   (c) Attempt to dismiss them all with a lordly wave of the hand;
   (d) Enquire who knows about beetroot production;
   (e) Catch the next plane out.

10. You are in Switzerland. The mountain guides pretend it is unsafe to climb the Matterhorn in a Force Ten blizzard. Would you:
   (a) Exclaim, "Dogs! Would ye live for ever?";
   (b) Say, "An Englishman expects every Swiss to do his duty";
   (c) Tell them about all the dragomans who were proud to drown for you in the Nile rapids;
   (d) Return, with a contemptuous shrug, to the Hilton;
   (e) Advance up the Matterhorn in carpet slippers, to teach them a lesson.

ANSWERS: *You are a man if you ticked the following:* 1 (*b*); 2 (*b*) *or* (*d*); 3 (*d*); 4 (*a*); 5 (*d*); 6 (*a*); 7 (*a*); 8 (*b*) *or* 9 (*d*); *All these courses are hopeless and the plane is fully-booked;* 10 (*e*).

The First Twenty-One Miles are the Worst

Cross-Channel via VINCENT MULCHRONE

I'D like to have it on record that I once crossed the Channel on two bottles of *Sancerre* because I was with Fred and I wanted to be sober when the party hit Boulogne.

To get Fred out of the way (not that anybody ever wanted to) he was a rather special Fleet Street character who was in love with his wife and the English Channel in roughly equal proportions.

His idea of a day off was to take the packet to Boulogne, lunch on *moules marinières*, pay enormous tribute to the French wine industry and, frequently, fall into a state of bliss across some cafe table in the main square.

Boulogne taxi drivers would find him there and, charitably, push him onto the last boat back across the Manche, confident in the knowledge (unusual in French taxi drivers) that he would pay the next time he came across.

A sort of club grew up around him, making an annual pilgrimage to Boulogne wearing ties inaccurately inscribed "Encore des Moules." The club, which met at Victoria Station, had but one rule —"No drinking before Herne Hill," a full minute's journey south of the Thames.

It all collapsed after Fred's illness. Convalescing at home, he got under his wife's feet a bit until she suggested that he should complete his recovery with a week in Boulogne.

Off he went, booked into an hotel, made his usual rounds, fell asleep at his usual table, was picked up by an amiable taxi driver and loaded aboard the last boat to England where, at 2 a.m. in Epsom, he had the utmost difficulty in arousing his wife and persuading her that he was, indeed, her Fred. The next day he went back to Boulogne for his belongings, but things were never the same again.

A pity he didn't live to read *Cross Channel** in which another Channel-lover has chronicled the comings and goings—quite extraordinary when you consider it's only 21 miles of water at its narrowest—across one of the most compulsive stretches of water on (or, obviously, slightly below) earth.

I had always thought that the compulsion to master the Channel reached its peak in the summer of 1875 when Captain Matthew Webb, anointed with porpoise oil, and occasionally sustained with British beef tea and strong ale, swam it.

Or was it—author Richard Garrett raises the niggling doubt—an Italian called Jean-Marie Scarlatti, who served under Napoleon at Waterloo, was captured and interned in a hulk moored off Dover and, one night, escaped and swam back to Boulogne?

No matter. All the one-man-against-the-sea crossings seem to me

Cross Channel by Richard Ganett (*Hutchinson*, £3.00)

to pale against that of the hero who conquered the Channel with a sail attached to his foot.

Five months before Captain Webb began to reek of porpoise oil, a Captain Paul Boyton, of the United States Atlantic Life Saving Service, set sail from Dover in an inflatable rubber suit.

He didn't swim. Instead, he had a tiny mast fitted into a socket in the sole of one foot of the suit, from which was slung a pocket-sized sail controlled by lanyards.

He carried a paddle to act as a rudder, smoked several cigars and drank not a few brandies served from an accompanying vessel, and gave up a few miles out of Boulogne because, in the dark, nobody on the pilot boat could agree where it lay.

But, a couple of months later, his foot sail spanking merrily, he made it back to England and, for me at least, Captain Webb will never be the same again.

You'd have thought there were no new ways left to cross the sliver of water. But only last year a citizen of Penge attempted it in a wardrobe. And a jolly good wardrobe too, when you consider today's workmanship, because it took him three miles before he sank.

I'm still proud of my two bottles from the Loire, but they don't compare with the feat of a seaman called William Hoskins, who floated from Dover to Calais on a bundle of straw. Of course, they don't make straw like they used to in 1862.

It's been done on a tractor (1963) with the large rear wheels supplying the buoyancy and, in 1966, on a bedstead floating on oil drums.

All these are mere fripperies on more serious Channel business. Apparently it had a regular ferry service between Dover and Wissant running about 350 BC, which is more than you can say for AD, when strikes were invented.

In 55 BC the Romans tried it, not so much, apparently, to conquer the inhospitable island as to neutralise it during the Gallic wars. But they lost their cavalry and landed seasick anyway, lacking the advice of a 19th Century contributor to the *Illustrated London News*, who advised "three drops of creosote on a lump of sugar, taken two or three times during the voyage." (Had everybody taken his advice we might, by now, have had a perfectly good road across the Channel).

After years of peril by storm, privateering, and races between early steamships—some of which missed the boat trains of competing railway systems—the journey was so settled that, by 1884, a gentleman could take a train from Charing Cross at 9.30 a.m. and arrive at the Gare du Nord at 6.25 p.m. Much, in a word, as today.

Until the early years of this century, First Class passengers across the Channel could enter the United Kingdom without a passport, whilst steerage passengers could not. It was a measure partly designed to keep prostitutes and criminals away from Albion's fair shores, and was changed only when Albion found that these were precisely the people best able to afford to travel First Class.

Then there's your actual Channel Tunnel, an idea which may yet

"I'd like you to meet my dinghy."

celebrate its 200th anniversary without having bored beneath the Channel (not to mention those above it) more than 2,000 ft. in either direction.

In 1802, a Frenchman called Mathieu proposed a tunnel in which carriages would be hauled by teams of horses, changed in laybys at five-mile intervals, the whole to be lit by thousands of candles.

A later scheme proposed a tunnel of iron tubes, suspended from buoys on the surface. Yet another argued that the force of gravity would propel carriages to the lowest point in Mid-Channel, and even part way up the far slope, where an "atmospheric device" would suck them into France.

Not all the French were keen. As a summary of the time put it, "Frenchmen travel for pleasure, and London is not a city of pleasure. Its Sundays are dreary, its fogs repellent, and it requires some knowledge of the place to pass one's time pleasantly there even on weekdays."

Victoria and Albert were all in favour. To assuage British fears, French engineers proposed methods to flood the tunnel. Sir Garnet Wolseley, Commandant at Dover Castle, opposed the measure "intended to annihilate all the advantages we have hitherto enjoyed from the existence of the 'silver streak' "—his invariable term for the Channel.

So he had the approaches at Shakespeare Cliff, the air compressor stations, the hydraulic lift, and the mouth of the tunnel covered by heavy guns to meet the first French day tripper—much the same welcome, in essence, as he gets today.

Then, in 1909, at 300 ft. and 45 mph, and for two £500 notes offered by the *Daily Mail*, Louis Bleriot flew the Channel. Ten years later the first aircraft to make the scheduled London-Paris journey—and a nonsense of the Channel—carried one reporter, mail, some Devonshire cream and a few brace of grouse.

The garbled weather report handed to Captain Bill Lawford promised "Bolsoms in Channel and squaggy." The latter he correctly guessed as "squally."

To this day Bolsoms have not been sighted. But it's best to take your creosote just the same.

39

Following In Fodor's Footsteps

with views of Fielding, Egon Ronay and the Michelin on the way, ROBERT ROBINSON leads a tour round the guide books.

THE world of the guide book is not the real world. "*Bulgaria is a country of happy laughing people*" was the sentence which jumped out of an OBSERVER travel supplement not long ago and brought the whole thing into sharp focus. Wasn't there just *one* Bulgarian who was inattentive to the best interests of his employer, glum when there was nothing or the telly, prone to elbow beggars into the gutter crying "Thy bitch of a mother!", and even running up down-escalators in fits of pique? Or did you really have to fight your way through a merry rout of Bulgarian customs-officials, all with sunflowers growing out of their backsides, too busy chalking hopscotch courts to mark your luggage?

Digging into Temple Fielding (**Fielding's Travel Guide To Europe, 1973**) I get the same sensation that my £4.50 has bought me admission to Arcadia. The British "*are a handsome sturdy people, clean-limbed, clear-skinned*" (a proposition re-inforced by the single exception to it, a disc-jockey of my acquaintance whose face appears to have been pushed up closer to his nose on one side than on the other, and whose limbs, since he bathes regularly at Lady Day and Michaelmas, may possibly be clean, but must certainly be shiny), led by a Queen who is "*a great human being*" and ever in the van when it comes to "*splicing ropes in Girl Guide camps*", though she also likes to reserve time for her slightly out-of-the-way hobby of "*sampling puddings in a farmer's kitchen*".

Small wonder the Briton stands revealed as "*childlike*" for he has this "*charming, puckish, stubborn refusal to grow up*". As an instance of the latter, you might recall John Fothergill who ran the Spread Eagle pub at Thame. He used to put five bob on the bill if he didn't like the look of you—he called it Face Money. I wonder if Temple ever ate there? Our guide adds (and not a moment too soon) that "*khaki is local slang for horse manure*" and I'm glad he said it, otherwise I'd have had to.

Eugene Fodor, editor of **Fodor's 1973 Guide To Europe**, I take to be an enormous Scandinavian, fond of practical jokes (resist any suggestion that he is a wizened Viennese whose collection of violins fills a whole turret). *He* accepts the contradictions of travel writing with a merry gurgle, quoting the Scotsman who said "*Even in winter, Copenhagen is an ideal summer resort*", and comparing it with the Dane who claimed "*Denmark was never intended to be inhabited in winter*". "*So much,*" carols the excellent Fodor, his laughter echoing round the fiords, "*for the ambiguous nature of reality.*"

Fond of updating other chaps ("*Denmark, the last place in Europe*", writes Negley Farson, "*where sanity survives.*" No, no— "*the only place where sanity has yet occurred*" yodels the happy Fodor), he takes his own liberties with nature, and though he's got the vibes right when he describes a certain night-club in London as being "*a cozy spot with dim lights and hostesses*" (i e. neither the lights nor the hostesses are as dim as the clientele), I reckon the ambiguity is accidental when he says English girls' complexions are "*brought to perfect bloom by the moist climate.*" He's got them mixed up with the cabbages, as many a good man has before him. Interesting to note that Fodor finds Britain the best place in the world for what he calls "*junque*"—as for "bunque", go no farther than the travel guide itself.

There are two kinds of tourist. One seeks a higher standard of living than he enjoys when he is not on holiday, the other seeks a satisfaction from other people's food and drink that he has never found in his own. (Both categories, by the by, should be sharply distinguished from the *traveller*.) In pursuit of this chimera, the second chap has his fantasies titillated by a whole library of table-erotica, a pornography of the belly among which there is but one unimpeachable exception—**Michelin**. Food causes no rush of custard to the adjectives in MICHELIN, the business of eating well is treated as cold-heartedly as though the compilers were instructing in matters as literal as the changing of a wheel.

No rhetorical puff-pastry here, simply the exact price of one half carafe of open wine, the bleak injunction "*place the Guide upon the table*", a tally of specialities, and a classification that presumes you know that the mere *inclusion* of an hotel or restaurant has exercised the wintry discretion of French inspectors whose bias is towards disenchantment, who have reluctantly admitted, rather than, enthusiastically endorsed. The MICHELIN guide does not have its equal.

At the more eccentric end of the foodguide shelf (madder than Egon Toast, I'm sorry I'll write that again, Egon Ronay, and the percentages he awards in his DUNLOP GUIDE, infinitely more specific than Ashley Courtney and the booming generalisations to be found in his LET'S HALT AWHILE IN GREAT BRITAIN—strange title, that, as though the impetuous Rover-driving purchasers were to be restrained in their headline twenty-eight mile-an-hour dash through Devon), I say more whimsical, but with its own brand of reliability—based on the supposition that if lots of the right kind of people like the food, it's OK—is **The Good Food Guide**.

Often guilty of anthropomorphism—"*chocolate pudding dark as a Mahler Symphony*" etc—it is also given to downbeat opening paragraphs which makes the joints it recommends sound like haunted houses. "*Although the waiting is slovenly (when a member asked for the manager he was invited to try and find him) and there have been complaints not only of canned music but of a canned chef, nonetheless Major Rhomboid (who insists that guests wear regimental ties and refrain from smoking until he has proposed the loyal toast) is capable of producing a meal that is, in its own way, Tolstoyan—slow, remorseless, terribly Russian . . .*" Strange to say, these gloomy prognoses, instead of turning you onto dry toast and water for life, have provoked perfectly sane people (and I mean me) to drive across two counties to try the dinner.

As I say, not quite of this world. THE GOOD FOOD GUIDE and its style—academic though faintly trendy, as if a butt of colour-supplements had been leaked into the Oxford *fino*—is only a part of the fantasy to which all travel literature caters. I have a feeling no guide addict is ever disappointed. I'm not at all certain that people who actually *buy* guides ever go anywhere. I have a suspicion the dream is enough. If it isn't, you could always try the Park Lane Hotel—according to Temple Fielding "*a New Yorker raves about the motherly service she was given after suffering a fractured hip.*" Of course, if there's nothing wrong with you, stay right where you are.

"*As you may have guessed from your tropical kit, we are going overseas.*"

"Baghdad, and hurry!"

It's Quicker
by Red Carpet

That's LORD MANCROFT, that was

IT IS better to travel hopefully, Robert Louis Stevenson assures us, than to arrive. I have never yet discovered what induced him to make this asinine pronouncement, though I realise, of course, that he lived before the age of the Jumbo-jet, the Inter-city express, and the T. & G.W.U.

Hope nowadays tends to languish when Trans-Siberian Airlines regret to inform transit passengers of a further delay in the departure of their flight No. TSA 007 to Samarkand, and that this is due to operational reasons. (Operational reasons are to an airline what virus infections are to a doctor. You are to understand that neither of them has the faintest idea what has gone wrong.)

I doubt if R.L.S. ever had to sit for an hour outside Didcot station whilst British rail, reluctant to admit that in the winter our weather tends to be wintry, struggled to unfreeze the points.

No amount of graft or low cunning, no friends in high places, nor the lushest of red carpets will get you out of this sort of mess. There are, in fact, two types of red carpet, the one upon which your ego can pose with pride, and the other which may genuinely speed you on your way. The merits of the two must be separately assessed.

The first type of red carpet was designed to be laid up to the carriage door of some prestigious traveller by coach or rail; but even the best laid carpets can go oft agley. The army manoeuvres which King Edward VII attended in Yorkshire during the Summer of 1909 had to be cancelled because of the English Summer weather, and the King returned to Harrogate station before the arrival of the Royal Train that was to take him across to Sandringham. In his kindly way he tried to put the Station-master at his case, whilst that embarrassed official peered anxiously down the line, cursing the engine driver beneath his breath. "Tell me," said the King, "what will happen if, when the train does eventually arrive, the driver fails to pull my carriage up against the red carpet laid out here on the platform?" "Ee," replied the Station-master, tried beyond endurance, "Ee, let boogger try!"

Nowadays, the red carpet is seldom seen at railway stations unless you happen to be the sort of person who normally travels with four corgies. Privileges to a lesser degree, however occasionally, attend a Minister of the Crown. Once upon a time I was such a person, but it always worried me when, as I often did, I boarded a packed Cardiff train only to find that my secretary and I had been allotted an entire compartment to ourselves in order that we might discuss in secrecy the problems of unemployment amongst the slate-workers of Anglesey. No matter how much our unseated fellow-travellers shook their fists, mouthed insults, or scribbled obscenities on the steamy

44

windows, the guard refused to let them into our otherwise empty carriage. Some years later the improper thought crossed my mind that the guard, not sharing my political views, may have felt that all this parade of privilege could influence some votes.

That's one of the troubles about red carpets. The advantages they may bring to the beneficiary often seem to be at some other travellers' expense. "Good evening, Sir," says the air-line P.R.O., smiling a P.R.O. smile, "a pleasant trip, I hope. Here, let me take your passport." Since you travel widely and your passport is consequently big with visas, you must appear glad to be relieved of this heavy burden. You are whipped through Immigration at the speed of light, pushing aside elderly nuns and chronic invalids. You are hustled conspiratorially down long draughty corridors, and you naturally reach the baggage collecting area well ahead of the crowd. But your beautiful rawhide suitcase takes just as long to come out of the bowels of the airport as does the elderly nuns' shabby grip, and all you'll have gained is a swollen ego at the price of some nasty looks.

It's the same on board ship. You are nearly at New York's Pier 92. The baggage master, with a knowing glance, tells you that all is under control, and the Purser himself is looking after your papers. A private car has been laid on. Someone from the Consulate will attend. But as the ship is about to dock the familiar cry of "Everybody out" echoes along the quay, and a wildcat strike has you all, Duke and dustman alike, in its thrall. When it comes to carpets, the colour red means less than nothing to the unions.

The red carpet, however, means a lot to the aging film star who needs the publicity, and to the retiring ambassador who has lived on protocol all his life, and wants to savour it for the last time. Air and shipping lines have a private code with which they mark their manifests, in the same way that a tramp will mark a door for the benefit of the next tramp to come along. If, say, Lord George-Brown, or Mr. Mick Jagger are travelling with us on Trans-Siberian, it will be known to all concerned how they are regarded by Cunard and BEA. Thus the precise way in which the carpet should be unrolled can be the more readily assessed.

A general assessment is fast becoming more difficult to make not because docks, airports and railway stations are growing more comfortable, or their staffs more efficient, but simply because the sheer bulk of modern travel makes it impossible to try and separate the sheep from the goats. When Euston Station first reopened there were found to be no seats for passengers to sit on. This requirement had not in fact been overlooked. It was simply that the authorities didn't really want people to settle down and make themselves comfortable. They wanted passengers to come and go as quickly as possible, and thus make room for other comfort-lovers to take their place. They just wanted everyone to be equally uncomfortable.

In spite of this bizarre approach the travel authorities will never really run out of red carpet for the maimed, the sick and the blind, provided, of course, that they are given sufficient warning. What is actually wanted is a little less red carpet and a lot more good communication.

Couldn't T.S.A. have told me why my plane was delayed? I, too, am sorry that I was stupid enough to miss it when our flight was eventually called, but I'm not so observant as all those Pakistanis and au pair girls. The public address system is incomprehensible (even in English) and the closed circuit tv screen is practically invisible. And when I arrived, I know I hadn't warned anybody in advance that I'm badly lamed, but I wasn't lame when I disembarked from the aircraft at the end of a very slippery four-mile corridor.

I think all travellers should be regarded as VIP's and all should be treated to the red carpet. The motto of the Green Star Line was alleged to have been "Passengers must not," and there are still some carriers who regard the passengers as an infernal nuisance rather than as their source of daily bread.

Ideally, then, all carpet should be equally red, and it may have been the unlikelihood of achieving this Orwellian bliss that was at the back of Robert Louis's mind. If, however, that day ever comes there will still be some people who for one reason or another are desperate to work their way to the head of the queue. For them new carpets must be devised and old egos revalued. To those in urgent need of such preferential treatment, I commend a simple ploy. This calls only for the use of a small child, and the possession of an indelible red crayon.

Apply the latter to the face of the former in a series of irregular blobs. Then rub a moistened finger lightly over the face, in order to ensure uniformity. Grasp the child by the hand, advance boldly through the crowd looking neither to left nor right, but pointing anxiously at the child whilst muttering the word *Masern*, or *rougeoles*, or *morbilio* or *sarampion* depending upon whether you are hustling through Germany, France, Italy or Spain. At any harbour, station, or airport where English is understood the word "measles" will suffice, and it will prove an equally effective red carpet.

"*I take it you have a reservation.*"

"We must be nearly there—I can feel the savoir-faire."

THE EUROPEAN TOUR

More and more Americans are coming over to have a look at Europe before it becomes indistinguishable from America. MAHOOD records their comments

"I'm pooped—why don't you go out and shoot a few reels and I'll see it all at home."

"I somehow thought that Britain would be better under the Tories."

47

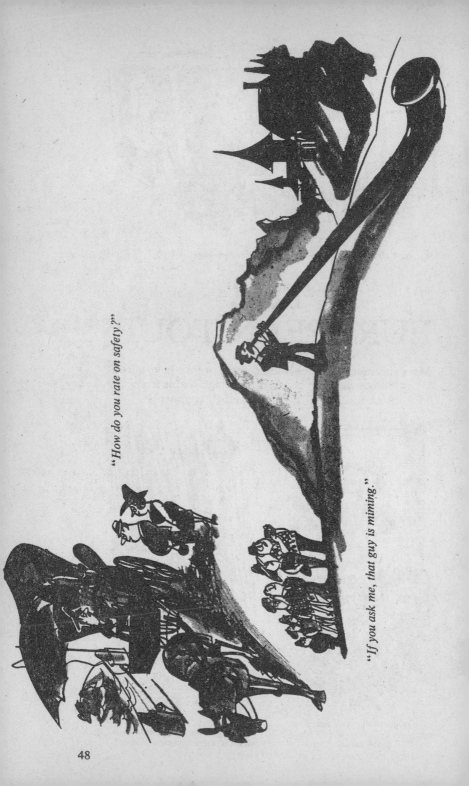

"How do you rate on safety?"

"If you ask me, that guy is miming."

"*I never realised what prime viewing
time could be like without the commercials.*"

"*Nobody sits anything out on our tours, Mr. Herman—
we insist that everybody gets their money's worth.*"

49

Cognac, Wednesday

by William Davis

IMPRESSED by the dateline, are you? Good. You are *meant* to be. Newspapers spend a fortune each year sending reporters around the world, in the unshakeable conviction that the people will admire their relentless pursuit of truth. The dateline is worth a wad of travellers' cheques: it proves that their chaps are actually *there*, even if they make their story up in some draughty hotel room. Mind you, it's got to be a foreign dateline. "Aldershot, Wednesday" doesn't sound nearly as good as, say, "Cognac, Wednesday"—unless, perhaps, you happen to be living in Cognac.

You may, of course, wonder what I am doing here, instead of getting beaten up in Chicago or observing our brave policemen at work in Anguilla. No, guess again. The answer is really quite childishly simple. As a connoisseur of datelines, I have always longed to put this one on my belt of scalps. But there is a more serious motive, too. I'm *waiting* for a story. If that sounds odd, let me give you a few facts of the roving correspondent's life.

You think he has a glamorous job, don't you? Wrong. Most of those fancy names on the map turn out to be a dreadful bore once you get there. And eighty per cent of a correspondent's job is drudgery—hanging around airports, battling with officials, checking into fifth-rate hotels, chasing leads, and getting one's story back to London. Especially getting one's story back to London.

There are, basically, two kinds of stories. The one you tell your wife, who sits at home fretting about the fabulous time she thinks you are having with some local floozy. The other is the one which your editor sent you to get for The Greatest Paper in the World. Both demand considerable ingenuity, and an immense capacity for hard work. Your wife won't believe that the town you are in is the dreariest place on earth, and that you've waited six hours for a telephone connection with London to tell her so. The editor won't believe that he was mistaken in his anticipation of a crisis, and that all the cable offices were shut when you arrived. He wants a scoop, and he wants it yesterday. This is why it's best to get to wherever you're going *before* something actually happens. Any fool can cover a riot or an invasion, but it takes real skill to be the only journalist in the right place at the right time—meaning at least twenty-four hours before your rivals even smell the story. It calls for a superior sense of smell, of course, and for a great deal of faith. But if it comes off, your reputation is made.

I have waited, patiently, in all sorts of places. I once spent three hours inside Vesuvius (yes, *inside*) in the hope that the damned thing would erupt, and that I could scurry down the mountain and tell the whole, harrowing, lava-stained story to an incredulous world. It didn't quite come off—Vesuvius managed nothing more than an unimpressive little hiss—but good reporters don't give up that easily.

I arrived in Cognac after waiting briefly in Bordeaux. I half hoped that lightning might destroy a year's supply of Château Mouton Rothschild, and I hovered around the Médoc for several hours, chatting up the *maîtres de chais* of all the big châteaux. Alas, the sun kept shining and I got nothing more than a bit of inside information: the '67 vintage is the best value for money you can get, and the '68 vintage is so awful that you'd be a fool to waste a single centime on it.

I moved on to Cognac, hoping for better luck. To the uninitiated, Cognac may seem an equally unlikely place to wait for a scoop. Most people, though, would have said the same about Anguilla a few months ago, wouldn't they? I caught a whiff, followed my nose, and here I am, determined to beat the world.

I hit town early in the evening, and made straight for that great fountain of knowledge—the nearest bar. None of my Fleet Street colleagues, I noted with satisfaction, had been blessed with the same brilliant inspiration. Cameron, Mulchrone, MacColl and the rest of them were all sitting at home, waiting for the editor's call, or roving around obvious places like Vietnam. Hardcastle, poor sap, had gone to Majorca. More encouragingly still, no one was distributing handouts. It makes one's job tougher, but a good story is worth a little hardship. I ordered a draught Guinness (yes, it's popular here) and addressed the natives in my best schoolboy French. You'd be astonished how many scoops have come out of a casual bar-room conversation. Some journalists never go anywhere else; they have nothing but contempt for over-eager cub reporters who insist on rushing about outside.

To my surprise, I came close to striking gold within a few minutes

*"The Peoples Republics are all very well, Adrian,
but it's the Fascists that get all the sunshine."*

of entering the smoke-filled room. Less than an hour ago, I was told, there had been an electrical failure at Courvoisier's vast Jarnac warehouse. The sparks *could* have turned the whole place into a blazing inferno. It does not require much imagination to see how the newsdesk back home would have dressed up the story:

PUNCHMAN IN BRANDY EXPLOSION

And beneath this banner headline, the coveted puff which precedes a real Exclusive:

Cognac, Wednesday

Millions of gallons of precious, forty-five-year-old brandy, worth a king's ransom, lit up the clear blue Cognac sky tonight in the most astonishing display of unplanned fireworks since Nero fiddled while Rome burned. A single British reporter was at hand to watch this historic event. He was, of course, the man from *Punch*—the only paper which gives you a *complete* coverage of major events around the world.

Alert warehousemen, alas, managed to deprive me of my scoop. The Norwegian managing director of Canadian-owned Courvoisier had the decency to apologise, and did his best to think up another crisis. He told me the Hongkong Chinese adored cognac (it seems to go well with sweet and sour) and that his whole stock would disappear in no time at all if ever Peking decided to buy the stuff. I said thank you, but I couldn't wait that long for a routine crisis. The near-explosion confirmed, though, that I was right to come here, and made me quite determined to go on waiting. *Anything*, after all can happen. And if it doesn't I can still fall back on the oldest rule in the book: "If there is no crisis, *create* one."

I could, for example, get myself arrested by the local gendarme. "Punchman clapped in irons by French Gestapo" wouldn't make a bad headline. (With luck, I might even get expelled.) All I would have to do is to stand outside the police station, and loudly proclaim the infinite superiority of whisky to the local brew. Somehow, though, I don't think I shall have to risk possible discomfort. I may stumble upon a less troublesome sensation—a bit of scandal concerning one of the world-famous cognac families, perhaps, or the discovery that someone has poured Andrews' Liver Salts into the precious vats. Meanwhile, I may compose a heart-rending background piece about the difficulty of communicating with London. If the Anguilla chaps can do it, so can I. The French telephone system, after all, is notorious for its inefficiency.

I hope I have said enough to convince you. This is a tough assignment—so tough that I would not let any of my staff touch it—and I don't want you to think that I am having a cushy time. My people in Tudor Street are calling it a holiday, but they'll stop laughing when they see my expense account. Hanging around in bars, drinking the stuff the locals concoct in ancient stills, is anything but fun. My hotel manager is suspiciously obsequious, the food is too rich, and I can't *bear* the spring sunshine. But as a hardened newspaperman, I'm not complaining. A story is a story, and long experience has taught me how to wait in silence.

Sometimes I Think He Understands Every Word I Say

*Accomplished linguist GEORGE MIKES tests
the ways to instant fluency.*

MY first sad discovery in the field of linguistics was that a foreign
language, alas, is not like influenza. You can't catch it just
by hanging around. You have to learn it.

The world has certainly changed quite a bit since the time I first
set foot on England (and, at the same time, England set foot on me).
In those pre-war days a large number of Hungarians (not speaking
of nationals of other minor races) were desperately keen on learning
English, the only language that mattered; today quite a number of
Englishmen are learning Hungarian and paying—according to the
prospectus in front of me—£719.40 for 200 lessons (including VAT).
In my days learning a foreign language was a pain in the neck;
today, teaching it has become Big Business. The schoolboyish
attempts of Englishmen trying to book a room in a French hotel in
pidgin French is a thing of the past, like the era of Palmerston.
Today aspiring but bored executives as well as diplomats flock in
their scores to language schools (it's almost 'a panic-stricken rush'
according to the *Daily Telegraph*) to learn not only the Common
Market languages but also such outlandish tongues as Norwegian,
Czech, Japanese and Urdu.

It was so much simpler and more leisurely in the past. When I first came to England I thought I knew English fairly well. In Budapest my English proved quite sufficient. On arrival in this country I found that Budapest English was quite different from London English—all the advantages being on the side of Budapest English. Here in England I found only two difficulties: I did not understand people and they did not understand me.

It was much easier with the written word. Whenever I read a leading article in *The Times*, I understood everything perfectly well, except I could never make out whether *The Times* was for or against something. In those days I put this down to my lack of knowledge of English.

The first step in my progress came when people started understanding me while I still failed to understand them. This was the most talkative period of my life. As long as I was talking, I was all right; the trouble only started when the other fellow answered. The next stage was that I began to understand foreigners but not the English (and still less the Americans). The most atrocious a foreign accent someone had, the clearer he sounded to me.

At the same time, my brother was struggling with the English tongue at the other side of the Atlantic. He was a believer in phrase-books and still has a formidable collection of them. In his favourite book the first chapter is headed: EVERYDAY CONVERSATIONS and the first question is this: "And how is Your Majesty this morning?" In Chapter Two there is a question: "Why is the Captain crying?" The answer: "Because his pen-knife is broken." My brother informed me, with great regret, that he could never ask His or Her Majesty how he or she was that morning and although he subsequently spent four years in the U.S. Army, he had never seen a Captain cry because his pen-knife was broken, I told him that perhaps the gentleman referred to was a naval Captain.

Another question (in one of his books) asked: "Excuse me, Sir, when does the next boat leave for New York?" The question was asked in Southampton and the answer ran: "In five minutes. If you run, you can still catch it."

My brother is still a believer in phrase books and keeps asking people—when he visits Southampton—about that next boat to New York. Once he was told: "Don't be a fool, you can't catch transatlantic boats as one catches a bus." My brother shook his head sadly. "That's not what you should say. You should reply to this question: 'In five minutes, etc'."

How do you expect—my brother asks most pertinently—poor foreign students to learn English if the natives pay absolutely no attention to the phrase-books and keep giving the wrong answers, not printed in them?

The days of this leisurely, nineteenth-century pace are over. Today tired and somewhat surprised executives are spending an enormous amount of time on learning Italian or Serbo-Croat, German or Malayan in 150 or 200 lessons. Or they take the "total immersion" course, from 9 a.m. till 6 p.m. every day, and even lunch with the tutor. A week of this costs £296.45 at Berlitz and six weeks of total immersion is no more than £1355.20. You hear (say) Urdu all day, you see Urdu, you smell Urdu, you dream Urdu but, in the end, you will probably speak Urdu.

This represents a shocking or, at least, a sobering change since those bygone days when shy refugees in London were coming to grips with the mysteries of the *th* sound and the intricacies of the English tenses. Today, if you want to export to Germany (and particularly if your business is such that you must talk to small, individual shopkeepers) you or your representative must be able to speak fluent and tolerable German because otherwise the Chap Who Has the Marks will buy from your Dutch competitor even if his goods are inferior as long as his knowledge of German is superior. It is sad that before we can export goods we have to import (or find) Finnish, Spanish, Hindustani etc. tutors to teach us those foreign lingos. (A language an Englishman does not speak is a foreign lingo; one he has learnt at the expense of £1355.20 becomes a language.)

All this may be right but I may be forgiven if I look at it with a certain amount of nostalgia for the past. When I became a British subject, India was—just for another few minutes—the brightest jewel in the King's crown. It saddens my heart to see those imperial colonisers busily learning Czech and being totally immersed in Urdu.

Sic transit gloria mundi—I say with a deep, nostalgic sigh.

And if you want to know what *that* means, subscribe to my total Latin immersion course, six weeks for £2127.83 (including VAT).

"*You would think that the idiots would have known by our G.B. plates that we drive on the* **left**."

How Good is Your Travel Talk?

Pit your wits against fast-talking E. S. TURNER

1. Grade the following remarks in order of phoniness:
    (a) "You can't beat a Latvian cargo-boat to Gdynia in March";
    (b) "If there's one thing I learned in Macao, it's never to refuse a squeeze of snake bile in one's drink";
    (c) "The hominy grits in Philadelphia are out of this world";
    (d) "Fancy spending £18 on three days in Majorca when you could give a couple of friends lunch at Robert Carrier's for the same money."

2. Which of these observations is most likely to halt a ladies bridge party:
    (a) "My husband picked up some sort of bug in Kazakhstan";
    (b) "My husband had all his ribs broken by a masseur in Istanbul";
    (c) "My husband got a black eye on the Burton's yacht";
    (d) "My dear, the Customs did things to me my husband never did in thirty years."

3. One of your dinner guests says, "We never did get to Florence, but we stopped off at a cute place called Firenze." Would you say:
    (a) "Oh really, how interesting?"
    (b) "More wine, anybody?"
    (c) "They're the same place, you twit";
    (d) "I remember looking for Leghorn and having to make do with Livorno."

4. Which of the motoring braggarts quoted below would you least like to know:
    (a) "You'd think they'd never seen a Jensen in Shiraz before";
    (b) "We bought a coupla new estate wagons in Stettin for the drive to Kiev and I reckon to ship them home from Odessa to Seattle for the hunting";
    (c) "If you think you're a good *corniche* driver, old man, try driving round the Corsican coast in an anti-clockwise direction in a hired left-hand-drive car at night."

5. Which of the following remarks is most calculated to whet curiosity:
    (a) "You'd never believe what goes on in those chiropodists' parlours in Bangkok";
    (b) "You'd never believe who was trying to thumb a lift on the M4, with her lady in waiting";
    (c) "You'd never believe what women used to get up to in the Red Sea";
    (d) "You'd never believe what they did to this pickpocket in Mecca."

6. Which of these openings is most likely to provoke physical assault:

(a) "When I was in Samarkand";

(b) "The first time I was in Samarkand";

(c) "The only time I was thrown out of Samarkand";

(d) "Whenever I pick up my car in Samarkand."

7. The man in the bar says to you, "Of course, you know that funny little brothel in Port-au-Prince?" Would you reply:

(a) "No, I'm a Trust House man myself";

(b) "No, but I saw the film *Belle de Jour*";

(c) "Yes, but you should have seen General Wang's brothel-car on the Mukden Express."

8. Which of these remarks elicits your sympathy—if any:

(a) "Six hundred miles from home and you have to order Ernie Marples's Beaujolais";

(b) "It always ruins my flight when they put me next to David Frost";

(c) "I happened to mention I'd been touring the game reserves and this little tick said, 'Have you seen Longleat?' ";

(d) "All I said to the crew was 'This is a hijack—ha! ha!' and they broke my arm in two places."

The reader whose answers most closely correspond to the list in the Editor's possession will receive a prize of Two Weeks In A Shared Bedroom in Staines.

" *I blame the tourists.*"

*"On the other hand, if they **did** make transistor radios,
I'm sure they'd make them very beautiful."*

Among His Souvenirs . . .

ALAN BRIEN forgets where he's been.

PERHAPS the most famous souvenirs to be brought home to Europe from the West were gold, the potato, tobacco and (some say) the pox. From the East, travellers brought back gold, silk, spices and (some others say) the pox. Not all proved to be what West End department stores at Christmas call, in their curiously mealy-mouthed way, "acceptable gifts". Still they proved that the giver had actually been abroad, which was presumably the original purpose of all souvenirs.

Today, of course, you invite Sherlock Holmes round to your chambers in Baker Street, to show him your snake-headed puzzle rings, your ebony elephants encrusted with tiny mirrors, your necklaces of silver temple bells, your brass studded belts indented with lotus patterns, your beaded caftans, your papier-mâché boxes with pictures of the Taj Mahal, your ivory fly-whisks, and demand— "Now then, Holmes, where have I been for my holidays?" And the great detective replies—"I should estimate you have travelled a mile and a half along the Northern railings of Hyde Park on the Bayswater Road between Marble Arch and Queensway."

The more attractive and genuinely indigenous the object you discover on your travels, the more likely it is to be available from the more enterprising retailers in your own native quarter. It will also be cheaper, less wearisome to transport, and less likely to fall apart as you unwrap it on the kitchen table.

If you want indisputable proof of where you've been, you must buy those goods that no sane Western businessman would dream of importing—and a right idiot you'll look in sandals carved out of old jeep tyres, carrying a suitcase beaten from petrol tins, wearing a djellibayah stamped "W∧D" or "Marshall Aid Programme", and humping a crate of cold tea in bottles labelled "Buckingham Place Wisky By Appointment to King Edward III".

You'd think one could bring back something from Vietnam to give the neighbours cause to talk—apart, that is, from an unfortunate rash, known as Saigon Rose, which curiously enough is now available in those anything-goes areas of Belfast frequented by foreign correspondents. But the Vietnamese markets seem designed to appeal only to those shopping for U.S. surplus war equipment to outfit a private army.

There is a general illusion among the stall-holders that all those inscrutable Westerners are clumsy, second-hand robots who will return to their hotels with large orders of radio valves, copper wire rheostats, hub caps, ammeters, cogs and pistons to give themselves a complete reconditioning and overhaul behind locked doors.

Eventually, I settled for a U.S. Navy hammock, a camouflage suit in pure silk with a battle map on the back, and a mobile composed of tiny tin pagoda roofs which tinkled in the breeze. And even the latter was partly made of Meccano and obtainable cheaper in Bangkok.

The first scrap-merchant to charter a freighter and begin combing the surface of Vietnam when the war ends will harvest a fortune. The ground sprouts with metal like dragon's teeth, and along the roads, like dirty milk bottles, are piled solid brass artillery shell cases worth at least £50 a piece. But what with the precautions against hi-jacking at all the major airports on the route home, I didn't fancy being shot out of hand for threatening the pilot with a concealed 150 pounder.

Even in Bangkok, a far more sophisticated city, the souvenirs are designed to resemble what Westerners sell in their antique shops rather than what the Siamese would sell in theirs. The clothes too are made up from beautiful soft materials but in patterns and sizes guaranteed to pop the eyeballs and cover the paunches of Miami Beach. I made the mistake, driven to frenzy by the heat, of stripping off my lead-lined jacket, so light-weight in London, and buying a gossamer shirt.

"This fit you, fit big man like me," said the huckster, himself the height of a British ten-year-old. I insisted on his "extra large outsize". He shrugged. I paid. He vanished. And I was left in a kind of Disney willow-pattern sampan sail, neck plunging to my sacrum, short-sleeves reaching my finger tips, patch-pockets covering my knees, like an infant struggling inside a grounded baggage balloon. "Medium", all over the East, now describes something even John Wayne's mother never thought he would grow into.

At least, in pandering to our tastes as tourists, most of the world provides some memento with a surface semblance of authenticity. It has local colour even if it does come off on your fingers. It pretends to have some use, even if you rarely want to comb your hair while taking your temperature and opening a bottle at the same time.

In London, wherever tourists gather together like fluff in a navel, the souvenirs are distinguished by their utter uselessness, by their air of being something you would only buy because you felt you ought to buy something.

Plastic, a material guaranteed to discolour, crack, buckle and blister but still outlast the Pyramids, is the favourite. Somebody sometime has moulded millions of baby dolls, and the same dimpled idiot face stares out at you whether dressed in a policeman's helmet, or a Highland kilt, or a Guard's tunic.

The magic name, outselling the Tower of London, the Houses of

"There they are, Sid . . . the good old white cliffs of Dover."

Parliament, or Buckingham Palace, is "Carnaby Street". You don't have to go there, though it may be around the corner, you just obtain a copy of the sacred words—on ash-trays, cushions, T-shirts, posters, street signs, Carnaby Street is Souvenirsville itself, and to have visited it by proxy is enough.

The area between Piccadilly Circus and Leicester Square now looks like a cut-price replica of New York's 42nd Street—novelty shops, amusement arcades, striptease parlours, pancake and hamburger houses. And the souvenirs are equally Americanised with only an occasional concession to Britishness. You can buy joke stickers, badges, labels and posters with slogans, like "Stop Pollution, Eat Garbage", which betray their trans-Atlantic origins in their vocabulary. The few attempts at specifically local quips appear to have been devised by those who speak our dialect only imperfectly, like "Knickers to Harold Wilson".

Last week, the longest queue was at a stall which sells "Your name in Headlines" for 39p a copy. And customers carried away, beaming, front-page news that Wong Ho Fook, or Gunter Grossman, or Jacques France, APPEARS NAKED ON WEST END STAGE! GOES ON WAGON; FIVE PUBS GO BROKE! VOTED PRIME MINISTER OF ENGLAND! or, inevitably, VISITS CARNABY STREET, LONDON! The souvenir is now fantasy— a tangible proof of something that didn't happen, which could be obtained by post without moving from home.

Just over the way, at the Design Centre, attempts are continually being made to improve the standard of our souvenirs. It attracts impressive numbers of visitors—last week, 37,873; last month 145,847. The current exhibition is called *Shopping in Britain*, and the quality of workmanship, design and materials is far superior to anything in the tourist traps.

But their association with the Britain in which the British live remains rather tenuous. When was the last time you went out looking for "Dressed Mice", for instance? Though this is apparently one of our flourishing cottage industries, and the address of the lady who assembles and outfits them is in itself a souvenir of a picture-calendar country—Mrs. E. M. Brickdale, Mousehole, Widford, Ware, Hertfordshire, tel: Much Hadham 2470.

Have you ever felt the need for an empty "effects box"? For a table lamp with the bulb removed which becomes a "pen store", for a Flickerbrick which is a "synthetic resin block with a long-life battery system and eight flashing bulbs" running for from one to five years "depending on ambient conditions"? For peg and marble games called "Nine Men's Morris" and "Fox and Geese"? What sort of Britain, part science-fiction lab, part Victorian nursery, would you be able to construct from this collection if you had never visited our shores?

Actually, I was very tempted to invest in several exhibits, particularly a Mamod steam traction engine. But it would be because I wanted the objects themselves for themselves (and for me) not as proof that I had been to their country of origin. The best souvenirs are souvenirs of you, not of your travel agent.

A Thinking Man's Guide to Paris

by FRANK MUIR

THE first time I saw Paris my heart was warm and gay, which dates it back to the days when 'gay' still meant carefree. I was rolling south in a clapped-out Frazer-Nash-BMW with one wheel-bearing crunching away like a coffee-grinder, driving my bride-of-a-day towards a month's honeymoon in Cannes on a travel allowance of £45 each. Another dating factor is that the problem then was not how to exist for a month on the Côte d'Azur for £45, but how to get hold of the £45.

The last time I saw Paris was last Spring, some twenty-three years later. Out-argued by my wife, son and daughter, I had allowed myself to be persuaded that their lives would remain shallow and meaningless until they had seen for themselves the Louvre, the Cluny museum, the Art-Nouveau Metro stations, Versailles, the Shakespeare Press bookshop, Notre-Dame, Chartres, the impressionists in the Jeu de Paume, and the hole in the middle of the rue Mazet where Magny's restaurant used to stand. So with jaunty hearts and a bottle of Eno's we set out for ten days of pounding pavements and marble-floored museums.

Our hotel, called Les-something-des-something-or-other, was in the rue St Honoré and had been a suave and plushy establishment round about 1922. Its amenities included a deathly-pale porter of great age, a sombre inner courtyard in which, during the whole ten days we were there, a portly American girl sat amidst fourteen pieces of luggage writing post-cards, a piano with inlay flaking off like sunburn, and a small framed card which read, *Menu: Potage du Jour. Gigot. Fromage. Fruit.* There was no dining-room.

Our accommodation was delightful; two large bedrooms, bathroom, and a tiny salon full of massive furniture which didn't open. Each room had a little frilly glass lampshade housing a Standard-Issue French-Hotel 7-Watt electric bulb. Each morning we had a decadent breakfast *en déshabille*, lolling about in our little salon and toying with our rolls, apricot jam, and coffee at blood-heat.

As the purpose of our visit was cultural I kept a detailed journal.

My jottings might prove to be of value to others contemplating an educational sojourn:

(a) No Paris taxi-driver knows where your hotel is. Or where anywhere else is. They don't know their Bourse from a hole in the ground.

(b) When you sit at a rear table in that café near the Madeleine and look down the short corridor leading to the kitchen you discover that a Paris waiter fully laden with a tray of dishes can, without slackening pace, in the space of six feet, take out a Gauloise, light it, take three puffs, nip it, select and entirely consume a hunk of food from one of the dishes, bend down and swig back a quarter of a litre of wine from a bottle concealed in a low cupboard, and comb his hair.

(c) When you are trotting down the stairs of your hotel and find yourself accelerating alarmingly because the treads slope downwards and you put a hand out to steady yourself against the wall and your arm goes through the plaster up to your elbow and you report it to the deathly-pale porter, he says "*ah, bon.*"

(d) When you undertake a sightseeing holiday on pavements you must steel yourself to the fact that you will not be able to take your shoes off even once until you get back home even if it means taking a bath face downwards with your shoes in the air because if you do kick your shoes off thankfully after your first day's walking you will not be able to get them on again due to the fact that once cultural-holiday feet are released from the discipline of being enclosed in shoes they balloon out in a matter of minutes into a shapeless mass not unlike leftover boiled pudding.

(e) When you carefully inspect the whole of the palace of Versailles and then foolishly decide to walk the fifty-odd miles down the garden to see the Petit Trianon and give up half-way down ill with fatigue and can't face toiling all the way back up and there's not a bus or a taxi and you stop a student driving a very ancient Citroen 2CV and try desperately to buy it from him, he answers with a short French word you haven't come across before.

(f) When you thankfully find one of the last genuine Parisian *pissoires* in the square opposite Notre-Dame and you are very tall and your head and shoulders rise well above the encircling protective metal screen and a coachful of jolly English tourists comes up not realising what you are about and ask you for your autograph, you haven't a hand spare to hold the book with.

(g) The sparks from French lighter-flints smell of garlic.

"Aha! . . . What's this?"

A PICTORIAL GUIDE TO AMERICA *by ARNOLD ROTH*

THE SOUTH

THE NORTH

THE MID-WEST

THE NORTH-WEST

THE WEST

Kindly Adjust
Your Dress
— or Else

NESTA WYN ELLIS looks at the Zanzibar fashion parade

IF you are planning a visit to Zanzibar pack a tape measure and/or a large enveloping cloak. Yes, it is the same Zanzibar, the one just near the equator, but if you think it's the kind of place where a fig leaf is overdressing, think again. Climatically you are on track, but take my advice, dears, fig leaves are not in style, and neither, selectively speaking, is flesh.

True, one fine day in Zanzibar you will see skin—demure glimpses. Faces, fingers and the odd ankle bone peeking out from under black or gaudy cotton shukas are all you can see of the birds. Anyone showing their knees and sporting a little white eyelet-embroidered pillbox is probably a man. But if you find unisex a problem, in Zanzibar you have a hard time identifying your friends. The long-term solution is to be an expert in lower leg characterisation and the individual aspects of toes.

This is no trendy fad, a product of some Zanzibari St. Laurent: rather the reverse—the anti-mode—devised not from the creative twirls of some fashion genius in a white velvet-panelled den with mirrored floors but by the Attorney General of Zanzibar. It is THE LAW no less.

From the hand of this five-foot Machiavellian sprite, a tiny black-eyed maverick who sits in a quaint old office for all the world like a set of the Middle Temple Chambers where he served his pupilage, has come a masterpiece—Revolutionary Council Decree no 1, 1973—that reads like a Wedgwood Benn policy document. Entitled, A DECREE TO SAFEGUARD NATIONAL CULTURE AND PROTECT IT FROM SUCH UNDESIRABLE FASHIONS IN DRESS, HAIR-STYLES AS ARE NOT CONDUCIVE TO NATIONAL CULTURE AND TO PROVIDE FOR ANCILLARY MATTERS THERETO, otherwise known as the National Culture (Protection) Decree, printed in typical HM Stationery Office House Style, this little document contains all the well-dressed Zanzibari needs to know to stay out of prison—or as the decree has it—a rehabilitation centre.

Naturally any visitor, tourist or traveller to Zanzibar will be anxious to fit in with local customs. In which case I would suggest they first locate their leg line. By this I mean, or rather the Revolutionary Council means, "an imaginary line drawn horizontally around the leg each point of which is exactly mid-way between lowermost part of the knee-cap and the uppermost part of the ankle." Aha. That's why you need the tape measure.

Having located your leg line, next turn to the bit that tells you what to use it for. I might add that there is no need, when first rising in the morning, to grope wildly for your leg line and ascertain its state of health (unless it so happens you are sleeping in a public place, and there is a regulation about that, too).

No, the main purpose of having a leg line featured on your anatomy is to avoid showing any flesh between it and your neckline—which for the purposes of your visit you should note is situated "one inch below the base of the neck". This applies to males, females and others.

It is an offence to reveal any supra-leg line physique when "standing, sitting, or lying down"—in which case lead weights stitched into one's hemlines would appear advisable—or to wear any form-fitting gear likely to reveal to which sex one belongs, or anything diaphanous. No hitching, twitching or flashing is allowed either under the heading "deliberate exposure", and we all know what that means, except here it means knees, elbows, tummies, the lot.

Screams of male chauvinism are wasted since the rules are as tough on men as women, although the male leg line permits shorts to be worn to "one inch higher than the uppermost part of the kneecap." Bodies, it would seem, are not quate nace.

To those who feel a visit to Zanzibar might be worse than a tangle with Savoy Hotel management I should, however, point out that there seems to be no objection to women wearing trousers. Men, though, must not wear "any pair of trousers which is tight-fitting or any pair of slacks which is bell-bottomed or flared". Why? Search me. If it's culture we are protecting, trousers are no more traditional dress in these parts than they would be in Scotland. Bells or otherwise.

Frankly, if I were drafting laws to protect national culture in Zanzibar I would be inclined to recall the delightful fashion in naked slave girls (and boys) and cash in with regulations more suited to the climate than all this bondage. (Just because slaves are no longer trendy there is no need to go to extremes.) Actually I suspect the Revolutionary Council of being fetishists who get turned on at the sight of two-legged bundles walking along with coconuts balanced on their heads.

As for male dress regulations, there I detect sour grapes. All the Revolutionary Council Members I've seen have been distinctly rotund: not the shape for loin-hugging bell bottoms. Loins especially seem on the black list and regulations for shorts insist that they "should not be so wide as to enable the loins to be exposed." Spoilshorts!

Clearly if anyone has in mind as a feature of their visit the sight of beautiful dark brown thighs of either sex they are going to be disappointed. The only place one is likely to glimpse them is on the beach of an afternoon when the entire male population of Zanzibar from the age of eleven upwards (dress regulations start to apply at ten) seem to be running up and down for all the world like mad dogs and Englishmen—engaged no doubt in some kind of physical training or else exulting in a clause of the law which allows a state of reasonable undress to prevail on beaches or during sports and athletics.

Women never appear on the beach. Hence the crowds that gather to view the exposed thighs (pale brown only) and bikini punctuated form of yours truly. Amazing how many Zanzibaris want to learn English and are clamouring to be taught how to swim.

Meanwhile when on the streets I do my best not to be offensive But really, darlings, what does one wear? I haven't a thing conducive to national culture in my entire wardrobe. As for the braless look, once swaddled up in your shuka no one can see whether you even qualify for the garment. All the more reason, you might think, for asking people back to see one's Zanzibar chest.

Worth considering is an escape clause which says that one's national dress may be worn without provoking riot, mayhem or arrest. Do short skirts, see-through blouses, thigh-slit maxis and topless tops qualify as National British costume? A test case is undoubtedly required. But rather you than me.

The law says you can get off with a caution for the first offence. On the other hand you might get your hair shaved off or be liable to corporal punishment of four heavy strokes or four light strokes or two light and two heavy. Further offences involve one in anything from six months to "an indefinite period at a rehabilitation centre". Since the Zanzibaris do not let the Red Cross or Amnesty International into their prisons I prefer not to take any chances on rehabilitation, thank you.

I would rather stick to the clause allowing one to wear whatever topless, see-through, bell-bottomed, skin-tight, mini garment as is one's wont, so long as the offending outfit is covered up with anything from a kanga, buibui, or shuka to a dirty raincoat. Hardly ideal for the climate but at least that enables us foreigners to get to and from each other's little dinner parties without fear of being delayed at an instant session of the People's Court followed by two years rehabilitation.

But however accustomed one becomes to checking one's leg line or wrapping old bedspreads round oneself before going out, there are times when one stops to wonder what it's all about.

In a climate where clothes are mostly superfluous all this cladding seems like evidence of a clothing manufacturer's lobby. Minis take up so little cloth compared to kangas, kitenge dresses and the like. Could the cotton producers have nobbled the Revolutionary Council, or might it all be part of a move to stop the flow of foreign exchange into a black market in imported looms?

Zanzibar, alas, is not the only place where you have to adjust your dress before leaving your aircraft. In Malawi, European women have to wear skirts exactly four inches below the knee: President Banda is reported to have thought maxis (widely worn after he banned trousers and minis) were a way of mocking African fashion. Apparently his view of what white mem-sahibs should wear dates from the days of colonial cotton frocks and crepe-soled sandals sported by leather-faced, loud-voiced ladies of the Empire.

Uganda's regulations, cobbled together Dada style a year before Zanzibar's, lash out, among other things, at hot pants, any wearer of which "shall be deemed an idle and disorderly person", sent to prison for three months and fined ten pounds. The leg line may be a liberal two inches above the knee but the policemen carry tape measures and make you kneel down on the pavement for spot checks.

Is all this puritanism in three ex-British Protectorates a gesture of contempt for the yoke of imperialism? If it is at times attributed to a renewed espousal of Islam however, there are elements in this strange cult for long dresses and high necklines which smack of early Christian missionary stuff.

It may be only thirty years or therabouts since everyone here was sensibly running round bare-arsed in the bundu—or shall we say naked in the Garden of Eden: and since then someone somewhere has been chomping at the fruit of the Tree of Knowledge.

I am reminded of the tale of the lady missionary in pre-independence Zambia who, shocked by the fact that the local girls wore no knickers, organised them into a sewing circle. The only snag being that once the frillies were finished, the girls, with typical African mischief, wore them on their heads.

"I still say a holiday at home is much better than Las Palmas—at least we've got the beach to ourselves."

Apres-Ski, Le Deluge

An Alpine trek with CHRISTOPHER MATTHEW in search of
packaged hedonism

IT was midnight in the Aquarius Nightclub in the French ski
resort of Les Arcs. I was standing by the bar in my fawn, camel-
hair, wrap-around overcoat peering through the smoke and the
darkness and the blare of music and the steam on my glasses at a
jigging, jostling floorful of readers of *Cosmopolitan* weekend *en fête*
(or on their feet, as we say in English). It was a fearsome sight. A
woman with eyes staring and arms outstretched gyrated wildly in
front of me singing, "Love me, baby, love me . . ." I declined the
invitation.

It was all, I reflected, a far cry from my first ever ski-ing holiday
fifteen years ago. Then I had gone with a school party to Soelden in
Austria. I had taken quickly and easily to skis, not to mention to
Jutta—blonde and beautiful from Karlsruhe. Every afternoon we
drank hot chocolate together and danced to *Volare*, and in the
evenings we danced again and caught greasy pigs and sat hand in
hand solemnly watching middle-aged Austrian gentlemen in leathern
shorts slapping each other's bottoms. I was surprised, I remember,
to discover that love fades only slightly slower than an Alpine tan.
Not so the memory, and just as Ronald Colman had to find that pass
back into Shangri La, so I too knew I had to get back to the mountains and re-live the romance of those 13 days for only £38. I did,
and have continued to do so ever since.

I have never quite succeeded in recapturing the magic of that first
Alpine encounter. Even so I can honestly say that not a year has
passed when I have not involved myself in some romantic derring-do
or other. It's not, you understand, that there's anything special
about me; any old Alpine hand will tell you the same thing—that
the chances of one's wildest dreams being realised on a ski-ing
holiday are traditionally a great deal higher than on any other sort
of holiday. Which was why *Cosmopolitan's* unequivocal offer of
"Three days of pure hedonism from only £28" had to be the last
word in ski-ing holidays. The magazine had joined forces with Erna
Low Travel Service and arranged a special January weekend party
in Les Arcs "so you can master the art of the slopes by day and the
après-ski by night." Ho ho. "A posse of handsome instructors will
be waiting to greet you and they're already taking a course of English
lessons to make sure they can communicate! It's impossible not to
make friends in a ski resort and there's always a healthy quota of
available men, so don't worry about coming alone . . ."

I had a vision of a solid phalanx of brown faced Frenchmen in
full ski-ing order braced, like an American football team, to with-
stand the onslaught of 120 liberated ladies as they sprang from the
coach like Greek soldiers from the belly of the Wooden Horse—
secretaries from advertising agencies, rich 40-year-old divorcees,

dress designers, fashion models, actresses—all without exception appallingly beautiful, and all intent on one thing and as soon as possible. I saw the confident grins of Claude and Jean-Pierre and Patrick and Giles turning into grimaces of fear as they were borne to the ground and thence away to hotel rooms and, in cases of extreme urgency, not even as far as that . . . It seemed so unfair that they should have to suffer alone, and I decided that I too should be there to play my part in ensuring that neither Erna Low nor *Cosmo* ran the risk of being sued under the Trades Descriptions Act. Confident of making a positive contribution to the proceedings I stepped into the Departure Lounge at Gatwick and . . . instant piece of Market Research: 50% of *Cosmo* readers are middle-aged men in dirty anoraks, and the rest are just like you and me.

Slightly shaken but far from stirred I asked one of the organisers if I could cast an eye over the list of weekenders. Each of the names had the letter A or B against it. Mine had B. She explained that this merely referred to the different types of ski passes, but I was far from reassured. Then a pretty dark haired girl opposite me leaned forward confidentially. "Actually they stand for ambidextrous and bisexual," she said. I felt a frisson of excitement run down my back, though it may have been that the cold air nozzle was badly aimed.

I saw the same girl later in the hotel corridor looking, like me, for her room. "I'm in 3197," I said lightly, dangling the key casually in front of me with the room number clearly showing, "3197." "Oh," she said, "in that case I'm definitely on the wrong floor."

The following morning I looked in on the ski school to check any likely competition from ski instructors and was delighted to discover that for once all that tired old broken English rubbish was not going down at all well with our girls. Later, as I took the lift up to the special Snow Barbecue I found myself remembering a film I had

"*I think, sir, you'll need a larger wallet if you're travelling to the States.*"

seen in Oxford ten years ago called *Nudes in the Snow*. It was a lovely film—all about these girls rolling about in the snow without any clothes on. The barbecue was very enjoyable too even though it did take place indoors, and even though the most I saw anyone peel off was a glove. The *on dit* amongst the *Cosmo* staff though was that everyone was getting together very nicely indeed, although there seemed little evidence that people were getting together any more quickly or easily than on any other ski-ing weekend. Some of us indeed had the distinct impression of actually drifting apart from the rest of the party. The moment had come to play my trump card—an exuberant, if at times somewhat unorthodox ski-ing style—and I invited the dark haired girl to join me on a brisk guided tour of the Les Arcs pistes. Unfortunately my newly hired boots rather played me up and I had to be helped down.

By the end of the day I was beginning to appreciate all those *Cosmo* articles on the fragility of the male ego. The highlight of the evening was a special screening of *Dernier Tango à Paris* (the original uncut, hot buttered bums version). Nervous at the demands that might be made upon my body at the subsequent *Glühwein* party round the Hotel Winston pool, not to mention the notable absence of the promised Instructors, I wondered if a more suitable film for readers of a magazine purporting to be about love and understanding might not have been *Escape to Happiness* with Leslie Howard and Edna Best—a conjecture that was later proved to have some basis in truth to judge by the fact that almost every member of the audience either left early or fell asleep. It was hardly surprising under the circumstances that the *Glühwein* party turned out to be exceptionally short on horseplay.

By the time I'd hired better boots the following morning, the dark haired girl had disappeared. I caught sight of her once in a ski class and ski-ed past, going particularly well, but she was busy looking at the instructor . . . So anyway, as I say, there I was in the Aquarius Nightclub. It was a pity really that I had missed the preceding Gala Fondue (or Fondle as it was already being wittily referred to), but I had been very tired after ski-ing. In a far corner I thought I could just make out the dark haired girl. The man she was with seemed to have very tanned skin and very white teeth. On the other hand it was very dark.

"You know what?" I turned to confront a blonde sporting a bouffant hair-do. "No," I said, "what?" "People who wear overcoats in nightclubs display a great lack of confidence." She reached for her drink, caught the end of her cigarette on my coat and burned a small hole in the belt.

The following afternoon Departure Lounge 4 at Geneva Airport was shrill with the traditional cries of the English splurging the last of their foreign currency at the duty-free counter. "(Darling, should we get a brandy just in case . . . ?") I stood with my hands deep in my pockets watching. Suddenly my zip flew open. A large man with his arm round a girl called out, "It's too late for all that now, cock." It was, much.

Still, I daresay I'll be able to weave a bit of romance round the burn in my coat if I put my mind to it.

ALAN COREN

Summer
in
St. Moritz

IT is the sheer altitude of St. Moritz that takes one's breath away.

"Twenty-five quid a *night*?" cried Dickinson.

A tiny porter tugged at his dapper leatherette hold-all, but Dickinson held firm. They rocked together on the foyer carpet, ankle-deep.

"Not, of course," and the Assistant Manager of the Palace Hotel opened a smile whose inlays could have wiped out the National Debt, "including breakfast."

"Naturally not", I murmured, being immeasurably suaver than cartoonists in general, and Dickinson in particular. I would have snapped my fingers derisorily, had they not for some unaccountable reason suddenly become oiled with sweat.

"That is the cheapest single," said the Assistant Manager. "If the gentlemen required something overlooking the lake, it would be two hundred and fifty francs per person."

"Ah," I said, "about thirty-five pounds, Geoffrey."

"I think," wheezed Dickinson, who had been dragged some way towards the lift by the uniformed midget, but had fought his way back, game though panting, "we ought to step outside and have a bit of a count."

"Ha-ha-ha," I said. It was the sort of laugh you say. "My colleague will have his little joke."

"Fortunately," said the Assistant Manager, "this is the low season. In winter——".

"Quite," I said. "What a bit of luck."

There was a discreet movement behind the AM, and an elegant vision materialised, offering his hand. Mr. Badrutt, owner of the Palace Hotel. There was a round of brisk bowing and nodding, not unlike that carried on by those birds you used to be able to buy who dunked their beaks in tumblers of water.

"I myself shall be in London next week," he said. "The grouse season, you know. We shall have grouse here on the thirteenth," he said. "A pity you will not be with us."

"Ah well," said Dickinson, "you win a few, you lose a few."

It wasn't a bad room, really. Its pokiness was relievable if you opened its little window. You could see the car park. I went next

door to see Dickinson's. With the hold-all in there, we were a bit cramped. His looked out on a fetching section of roof.

"What the hell," I said, "I've seen lakes before."

"Yes," said Dickinson. "Just think, we've saved twenty quid between us already."

I joined him, half an hour later, at the lift. He was looking particularly elgant, I thought, with an ochre stain the size of a soup plate on his shirtfront. During the titanic battle with the flyweight bellhop, it transpired, Dickinson's after-shave had broken free of its moorings and run amok among his smalls. If it could do that to poplin, God knows what it does to faces.

"We are after rich widows tonight, Dickinson," I reminded him. "Now that the ski-instructors have gone into whatever the opposite of hibernation is, there are breaches to be stepped into, not to say out of, and here you are smelling like a Turkish sweet-shop. Where's your other shirt?"

"This is my other shirt," said Dickinson.

The lift arrived, and we stepped in. There was a dinner jacket propped in one corner with a very, very old thing inside it. We said Good evening, in three languages, but it didn't open its eyes. It was croaking a bit, though, which suggested that something was struggling through its veins, however watery. When we reached the ground floor, the doors opened automatically, and, though they ignored us, two liveried bystanders sprang towards the tuxedo, thus demonstrating him to be an item of note. Before they could reach him, however, the lift-doors closed again, and he sank, motionless, out of sight, towards the swimming-pool. As one, the flunkies leapt for the stairs, in pursuit.

"It is the altitude," murmured the Assistant Manager, who had joined us, and was pressing his nose against the door-glass in the hope of catching sight of the lost guest, who turned out to be a Count not only von somewhere, but zu it as well. "St. Moritz is almost nine thousand feet above sea-level, you understand. For many of our older guests . . . "

In point of fact, the Count was one of the younger guests. For much of the next two days, Dickinson and I were constantly coming around corners of this elegant pub, only to find octogenarian European nobs leaning against the flock wallpaper and breathing what only a trained geriatrician would have been able to tell was not their last. It may well have been that some guests actually snuffed it during that time. It is a discreet spot, and no whisper of mortality would have been allowed to echo down its plush labyrinths; but there were two long, black, hotel Cadillacs parked outside the front door at all hours, with more than enough room in the boot, at a guess, for a Graf and a couple of shovels.

We did not wait for the staff to dredge our fellow-passenger from the depths. He was the wrong sex, and forty years too old. In search of bustier fellowship—something out of Lehar, perhaps, with a beauty spot and a dirty laugh—we sped to the bar. Was this not the bar which, at the height of the winter season, echoes to the laughter of Gunter Sachs, busting a gut over the latest Onassis witticism while all the Gabor sisters fight to autograph his plaster cast?

Perhaps. In summer, it echoes to the plink-plink of a waiter picking his teeth in an empty vault. We ordered a pair of dry martinis, and he crept away, leaving us with two hundred Morris chairs and our first view of the lake.

It must have been a nice lake, once. At the St. Moritz end of it, however, it now sported a flourishing village of cranes. As we watched, they began, very delicately, to build a pre-cast concrete skyscraper to put alongside its half dozen fellows. The late-afternoon sun flooded down the mountainside, and winked off the bulldozers; all very Swiss.

"There's not a bloody chalet anywhere," said Dickinson, who has an artist's eye for such things.

It was true. As we took in the landscape east and west of the site, we could see the whole of St. Moritz lying beneath us, like an Alpine Torremolinos.

"They'll have a job making cuckoo-clocks out of that lot," said Dickinson.

The barman returned with the drinks, and a bill for three pounds. The nuts were free.

"What do people do after dinner?" I asked him. I may have winked. Dickinson may have nudged.

"There is a piano in the main lounge," said the barman.

The pianist played *The Breeze And I* for two hours. Throughout this feat, he rocked from side to side, and never stopped smiling. It occurred to me that he was not a human pianist at all, but some masterpiece of the clockmaker's art; the lid of his grand remained shut, and I am of the firm belief that, had I found the temerity to open it, a life-size wooden ballerina would have sprung out of the innards and begun pirouetting until lights out.

She and her accompanist would still have had a thick edge on the other guests.

There were about a dozen of them, and they lay in their fauteuils like yellowed leaves from the *Almanack de Gotha*.

"If you laid them end to end," said Dickinson, "they'd stretch back to Hereward the Wake."

Why they had not hitherto been laid end to end remains a mystery: in the brief interstices in the pianist's lunatic recital, you could hear the wind sighing in their lungs like an aeolian band. Occasionally, a retainer would pass softly through, a nurse, a secretary, a chauffeur, and take a quick squint as if to ensure that his employment would last the evening. That they were loaded, there is no doubt. One old lady was ablaze from end to end with blue diamonds; she sat slumped in the middle of the enormous floor like a fallen chandelier, and every time she breathed, stilettos of light were hurled to every corner of the room. She was still there when, at last, we left; unable, I have no doubt, to get up under the weight of her mineral deposits.

Dickinson sighed.

"If she were eighty years younger . . . " he muttered.

At eleven p.m., we went to bed. The hotel was silent, the town was silent. I lay awake until the church clock opposite struck two. *The Breeze And I* was still tinkling away, somewhere far below.

What I awoke to in the morning was even odder. You recollect

"Would you mind sir—no wallets on the table please!"

that moment in *Treasure Island*, where Jim Hawkins first hears the approach of Blind Pew? Tap, tap, tap . . .

There must have been a thousand Pews outside. If I was any judge, there wouldn't be a household in St. Moritz without its black spot by sundown. I slid out of bed, and edged to the window.

Beyond the car-park, the street was alive with very old people in plus fours poking their way gingerly into the distance with their alpenstocks. It was like some mad attempt to make *The Guinness Book Of Records*. Where had they come from, where were they going?

The phone rang.

"They could be escaping from something," said Dickinson. "Maybe it's Euthenasia Day."

We dressed and went downstairs, and into the hot sun and the thin air, neither of which could have been too good for the citizens still filing past. And then we looked up, and saw that the hills were full of them: you could see their red socks everywhere.

"Afterwards," said the Hall Porter, who was standing on the steps beside us, "they go down to St. Moritz-Bad and take mud baths."

"It's the money," said Dickinson. "It softens the brain."

There were more old people at Silvaplana, four miles away, queuing for the cable-railway up to Corvatsch, a mountain-top where there is permanent snow.

"It won't be half as crowded going down," said Dickinson, his mouth wedged in my ear by the press of ancient flesh. "It's eleven thousand feet at the top. Maybe they go up there to die. Like lemmings. Maybe it's full of 'em up there, all frozen solid in perfect preservation, gazing out over the mountains they love, like Bird's Eye peas."

From time to time, in its upward amble, the cable-car would suddenly lurch to one side or the other as these well-heeled OAPs would take it upon themselves to fight to the window. Unable to fathom the activity, I put a polite enquiry.

"We think we see marmots," an old man said.

At the top, at last, we emerged onto a sheet of stone-hard snow. A few skiers, who must be addicted to the stuff, since there isn't enough of it to give even the tyro a run, were pottering about, but the bulk of the visitors were merely shuffling about in tin nose-cones, or lying around in chaises-longues and turning the colour of old wallets.

So we came down again. We had been away two hours; and for two return fares, two brandies, two coffees, and two chairs, we had forked out twelve pounds.

"I wouldn't care," said Dickinson, "I didn't even see a bloody marmot. Whatever it is."

"You know what I'm to do?" I said. "I'm going to take a mud bath. That's what I'm going to do."

But they didn't let me.

"You are needing a doctor's certificate," said the man in the downstairs hall of what might easily have been the world's largest mortuary. Huge nurses clattered about on the white tiling, dragging enfeebled citizens in voluminous bathrobes behind them. A man with a shower-cap pulled down over his eyes shot past in a wheelchair, going like Fittipaldi, with a huge retainer running alongside. Both weirdly, were shrieking with laughter.

"Come on," I said, "I'm half a century younger than any of this lot and fit as a flea."

"A flea?"

"It's an expression."

He shook his head.

"Your heart could go," he said, "pouf! Like that. You may, however, take a mineral bath, which can cure all known forms of psoriasis."

I know a bargain when I see one.

It was like hot Alka-Seltzer, and I came out feeling like a prune. I got back to the Palace somehow.

"You look terrible," said Dickinson.

"But free of psoriasis?" I enquired.

He stared at me for a bit, as a man will who has just blown a fiver on three large scotches.

"I've just twigged," he said. "They're not old at all, this lot. They just walk about on the mountains and take those bloody baths. They're probably not more than thirty, at the most."

We ate fondue, that night, in a deserted restaurant called Tavlos.

It's an interesting little ceremony, eating fondue and typically Swiss: you dip six little pieces of meat in a saucer of curried mayonnaise, and give the waiter a tenner.

While we were there, a man in lederhosen came in, pulling an alpenhorn. He looked at us, and went out again.

"Pity, that," said Dickinson. "I was rather hoping he knew *The Breeze And I.*"

It was nine-thirty, and the owner was noisily switching the lights out.

"It's been a fascinating two days," said Dickinson, just perceptible in the remaining bulb-glow. "What shall we do tomorrow?"

I opened our joint wallet to pay the bill. Out of two hundred pounds, there was just enough left to cover the imminent lodging.

"How do you fancy a trip to London?" I said.

"Will there be marmots?" asked Dickinson.

"It's a traditional melody—telling the people on the mountain that the pound has dropped again."

The Moon
and How Much?

by ALEXANDER FRATER (after Gauguin)

L AST YEAR I stopped off in Tahiti on my way to Australia, keeping my ticket open and my plans vague. For a day or so I just lay in the sun, breathing in that humid, scented air and swapping abuse with the posturing French matelots who kept leaping into the hotel pool and drenching my leopard-skin trunks. Then I hired a rusting Citroen and drove to Point Venus and Matavai Bay where Cook, pursing his lips at the sight of women offering themselves for fish hooks, had landed.

I drove to the Arahoho Blowhole and the Vaipahi Waterfall and the place where the Tahitians buried their queens and, everywhere I went, I kept running into old men who, for hard cash, preferably American, would reminisce about Gauguin. One claimed to have rescued him from a swamp, several had got drunk with him, knocking back absinthe like milk, another had posed on horseback for a picture and yet another claimed to have fought him for the favours of a woman; Gauguin, it seemed, was a sprightly and dirty fighter who favoured kicking his opponents in the throat. Those items, all rubbish, cost me eleven dollars, but I forked out happily. The man and the legend were exacting their tribute and I was positively eager considering my own unsettled circumstances, to pay my whack.

The evening, as I bowled back to my hotel, was balmy with flowers, and the glances of the Papeete girls had my pulse chugging like an outboard motor. I went for a swim, floating on my back in a sea of tomato soup and watching the sky assume the thrilling coronary flush that it invariably assumes here. Suddenly, slightly to the west of me, a man emerged, wheezing, from the deeps.

"Oof!" he said. He was rum-coloured and wrinkled and he wore a glass mask full of water which he removed to reveal a pair of myopic but benign blue eyes. "I saw something down there," he said. "I bared my teeth at it and it swam away. It may have been my wife. She is still submerged. She has the lungs of a bull walrus. I am Dr. Bonesera, by the way. I teach Latin at the Lycée. What are you doing in Tahiti?"

"Actually, I'm not entirely sure," I said.

"Are you an artist?"

"God forbid," I said, but I found myself telling him, after a companionable silence, about my, um, novel. I had started it in England and then run out of steam. The thing refused to gather momentum. I felt debilitated and intellectually undernourished and little things got on my wick. The milkman kept smashing bottles outside my window. The central heating started making a deep Wagnerian hum. The manic dentist next door bought a bugle and played it in the garden while his mistress, Virginia, raised the flag.

The weather was bleak and the economic situation depressing. My friends, gloomy about rising prices and falling property values, regarded the writing of a novel as frivolous and became overtly hostile. Everything seemed to conspire against me. I had put my skimpy manuscript aside and, with it, my aspirations. My life was clearly destined to contain no monuments but, that afternoon, I had felt my muse starting to thrum. Snatches of dialogue ran through my head—a sequence of grunts, mostly; the book was about a recluse who shared a cave with a tribe of seals—and I felt that heady soaring of the spirits that denotes the anticipation of good work to be done. I mentioned this to Dr. Bonasera and he showed no surprise.

"Then clearly you must stay and write your book here," he said "Tahiti affects certain temperaments that way. It strips away the, cladding of cold climates and leaves the creative centre exposed and sparking." He clearly felt very proprietorial about the place and ten minutes later, as we dog-paddled back to the beach, trust established, friendship blooming, he said he had a shack in the hills and it was mine for as long as I wished. I demurred. He insisted! We went and had a gin. "What about your wife?" I said, after the third. "Shall I order for her?"

"She will be drinking further down the coast," he said. "Probably with sailors. And now pay attention, please. I will draw you a map. And I will put in the village, a kilometre from the house, where you may find a woman. She will cook for you, and take care of all your needs in the local manner. That is imperative if you are to work well."

Next morning I drove into the hot, shimmering hills and found the place, a sort of abandoned stockade overgrown with vines. They covered the door and windows and the light within was dimly green, rather like being underwater. It was quite habitable, though, and I unpacked and got myself established. The view was very fine, sea mostly, and I watched an aircraft carrier traverse it in 29 minutes. Then I got to work. The story needed some love interest. After several hours thought I introduced a whale which swam into the cave of Figg, the recluse, and got stuck. This seemed quite promising and I typed hard for nine minutes while the sweat coarsed between my shoulder blades and a goat walked in and ate a tennis sock. I drove it off with a barrage of lemons, lunched on cold baked beans and went to sleep.

That evening I went to get myself fixed up. The village consisted of huts grouped around a Chinese store. I bought some beer, sat on the stoop and drank it. There were plenty of women in evidence, but they moved about with a purposeful air and had the sort of build that went with felling trees and damming rivers. I was just about to give up and go home when a girl in a white sarong loomed up through the gloaming and sat beside me. I stole a sideways look at her. Her profile was sculpted, her manner grave. She wore a white gardenia behind her ear and the scent she gave off—ylang-ylang?—strummed at my senses like fingers on a lute. "What do you think about The Bomb?" she said.

" Your perspective is a bit out."

"What bomb is that?" I said.

"The French bomb.' she said. "Our bomb."

"You mean they keep it here?"

"Right in the middle of Papeete," she said, "if the rumours are to be believed. Some say it is hidden in the cathedral, guarded by priests. Others say it is in the Attorney General's wine cellar. I have even heard it said that it is to be found in a certain brothel, near the waterfront. We do not know. But we are organising ourselves. We are starting to protest. Will you join us? We are going to storm the Governor's Residence. We will plant yams in his tennis court and blow up his swimming pool and tell him to take the damn thing home and drop it over the Camargue."

"I'm with you," I said.

"Good." She took a paper and pencil from her pocket. "This is our petition," she said. "Sign here, please."

I signed and then, because these Polynesian women don't muck about, I came straight out with it. Would she, I asked, care to share my bed, cool my beer, skin my quinces and lead me to Mass on Sundays? I beamed at here, ingratiatingly, while she simply stared. Then, in a rising contralto, she called me a chauvinist pig and went for me with her petition. I prised her hands away from my carotid artery and sloped back to work.

The work was not going well. Figg and the whale were establishing a rapport, but slowly. I didn't like the whale very much. It just lay there, with its eyes narrowed and its lip curled, demanding that Figg swab its back and blowhole with cold water. Each evening I went to the Chinese store and talked to women. I explained my needs and circumstances and told them that if they wanted a minor classic devoted to them, the most moving and incisive exploration of a man's relationship with a whale since *Moby Dick*, all they had to do was follow me home through the trees. They assumed I was being droll. Only one, a physiotherapist, stayed a while to talk. She had recently attended an international symposium on rickets in Maracaibo and she expressed some concern about my posture. "Do you always sit with your legs crossed?" she said.

"Yes," I said. "Most of the time."

"Tightly?"

"Quite tightly."

"That is very bad for your spine," she said, and made me sit up straight before she left to cook her husband's dinner.

On the fifth day I drove to an escort agency in Papeete. The book was at a virtual standstill and I was sleeping badly. A thin, red-headed woman with large hands asked me what I wanted.

"I would like to meet a nice Tahitian girl," I said.

"We don't have many actual Tahitians on our books," she said, "but I can do a nice Australian scuba diver. or do you prefer them French? I've got a heavy water expert from Calais, brown eyes, interests ballroom dancing and pottery. I can do a Brazilian divorcee and a resting go-go dancer with a sprained knee. If you like them Japanese there is the skipper of a refrigerated fishing vessel who wears Thai silks and claims she is a woman though her dates often complain about her tattoos and the fact that at midnight she leaves them to shave. But she waltzes beautifully and I'm told that . . ."

I thanked her and retired. In the street, looking for a bar, I saw an airline office instead and asked about flights to Sydney. There was one leaving that evening, dinner served after take-off, a John Wayne movie later, and I booked. In the Departure Lounge I was approached by an official who said she was doing a survey for the Tahitian Tourist Bureau. Her teeth and eyes shone, and her uniform celebrated the sort of body I had fantasies about when my voice was breaking. "Gauguin should have painted you," I said.

"He painted my grandmother instead," she said. "What was the purpose of your visit, please?"

"I was trying to write a novel and form a liaison with, uh, a woman."

She noted that down. "And?"

"I have finished seventeen pages and broken out in a rash I can only attribute to gloom."

She glanced about nervously and made a hushing sound. "Please mention that to no one," she murmured. "Such reports would be very bad for Tahiti. We must protect our reputation at all costs. She jotted a name and number on the back of a card. "Here," she said. "When you return, call me and I'll help you finish your book. Have a nice flight."

I haven't been back, but I still have that number. If anyone is planning a trip to the South Seas, I can be contacted care of this office. The price, of course, will be subject to negotiation.

And I'd like to roll to Rio, Some day before I'm old!

Seven writers dream a little dream

Frank Muir

IN considering my Dream Trip, or indeed any trip, I am not so much concerned with the *where* as with the *how* of it. R. L. Stevenson's noted remark that it is better to travel hopefully than to arrive makes sense if you are astride a donkey but is an appalling thought if you are encapsulated in a Trident at forty-two thousand feet.

The fault, dear BEA, lies not in my airline but in myself. This I know. But I do think that if God had meant me to fly He would have given me a smaller body, as well as more money. If my literary stoop could be ironed out I would stand six-foot six high and in order to accommodate all this into the space alloted to Tourist Class clients I have to arrange myself into a kind of foetal crouch; an ugly, tedious process like trying to cram a swan into a carrier-bag.

Once airborne I sink into a weird, coma-like trance. All mental processes cease to function and the mind floats about in a state of suspended apprehension. I have been known to look at my watch a hundred and thirty-four times between flying over the Staines reservoirs and the Normandy coast.

My Dream is to turn up at Heathrow and be mistaken for Richard Burton. (Not impossible. Once, at an oculists, a lady mistook me for Barbara Cartland.) Commissionaires in white gloves would park my car for me, a senior official would take my ticket and passport away for processing and I would be hurried to a small room away from the hurly-burly and be persuaded to accept eight of nine glasses of Dom Perignon. A small car would take me out to the aircraft. At the top of the ladder I would be welcomed aboard by the chief stewardess, a recent Miss World, who would be proudly accoutred in see-through gabardine. Drawing myself up to my full height in order to acknowledge her greeting I would then crash my head into the top of the metal doorway and drop, senseless, at her feet.

I would recover consciousness just as the aircraft drew to a halt at our destination, the stewardess forcing five-star Duty-Free between my wan lips; all flying flown.

It's the only way to go.

Humphrey Lyttelton

IT'S predictable that a chronic jazzophile should opt for a safari along the jazz trail from New Orleans to New York. But don't give me a conducted tour. I want to be free to probe into the dusty corners where jazz legends have lain undisturbed for decades. I want to stand on the spot, on the banks of Lake Ponchartrain across from New Orleans, at which Buddy Bolden's cornet could be heard in Basin Street fourteen miles away on a clear night. I would love to interview some ancient survivor who was actually in Basin Street on one of those memorable nights, tho' I fancy he might be too impenetrably deaf to hear my questions. I would like to see—and hear —the telegraph pole against which the marijuana-crazed Leon Rappolo would rest his head, weaving a counter-melody to the humming wires on his clarinet. Most telegraph poles I know play a pretty dull tune, so this one must have been something else. I want to prowl the quarter deck of a Mississippi river boat at dead of night, hoping to meet the ghost of Emmett Hardy, the legendary inspirer of Bix Beiderbecke who is said to have played the cornet till his lips poured with blood. (Awkward query: Do ghosts bleed?) In Chicago I'd like to visit the studio where in 1926 Louis Armstrong dropped the words of "Heebie Jeebies" in mid-recording, scrabbling for the sheet music on the floor while at the same time inventing "scat-singing" for posterity. And in New York I shall have tea with the lady into whose lap the prodigious Johnny Dunn once blew a trumpet mute through sheer lung-power. Fancy if she turned out to be the same "What is jazz?" lady to whom Fats Waller and/or Louis Armstrong said "If yoh has to ask, lady, yoh ain't got it." I should be so lucky.

Alan Brien

IT should start with a Rolls at the door. Out gets the travel agent with a notebook—yes sir, fix that smell in the downstairs' euphemism; repaint the children's bedroom, yes sir; complete your income tax returns, sir; polish off those almost-finished articles, sir; answer all your correspondence, yes *sir*. When you return, a year's procrastination will have been wiped away, or your money back.

Drive to Westminster Pier, where the largest yacht ever seen by the Thames Conservancy is steaming at anchor. A real, old-fashioned, *Gentlemen-Prefer-Blondes* send-off, champagne, flowers, brass bands, tears on the landing stage, and all, including a few suicidal blondes and brunettes. Hooting away into a starry, silky night.

Dawn landing on your Dorothy-Lamour island (Dotty herself, untouched by time or Bob Hope, still the best *lei* of the Aleutians, dressed in a garland and a smile, waving from a palmy hill top where the natives drag you, tenderly, ashore in their canoes. You can walk round the fearsome, but safe, cliffs in a couple of days—would you believe forty miles circumference? The beaches would take six months to explore.

One walled city, too small to need cars, full of attractive, happy, prosperous *cafe-au-lait* (the best *lait*, etc.) citizens in a permanent state of fiesta. A language you don't feel ashamed not to speak, but like English with a comic accent you can learn in a day. A hotel with a room on stilts out in the bay. No papers but all news transmitted by gossip over drinks. Drinks like childhood lemonade, but non-fattening, and alcoholic without hangovers. Food like fish and chips, but non-dyspeptic, and in every possible flavour. Ancient remains, only half excavated, where you can find a gold necklace by digging with your big toe. A volcano which erupts only at midnight pouring a ration of lava safely out to sea. Weather warm, but not too sunny, or sunny, but not too scorching.

I don't know who arranges such holidays. If I did, I wouldn't tell you. After a month, they elect me mayor, or even god, and I never come home.

Michael Parkinson

I'M useless at dreaming. Faced with questions like: what would be your perfect holiday, or what six things would you take with you on to a desert island I assume all the qualities of a deaf mute. As a matter of fact I was recently asked that last question by another magazine. I thought for days about what six possessions I might take with me on to my desert island. It was only when I settled finally on the latest Wisden, Georgie Best's Soccer Annual, a distillery, an ice-making machine, the Pirelli Calendar and a signed photograph of Jane Russell I realised what a shallow person I am really. When the man rang me back to get my list I told him I didn't wish to be associated with his silly scheme. Some time later I saw they had put the same question to Alan Whicker and he had asked for six beautiful girls. Now why didn't I think of that?

So where do I want to go for my dream trip? Well to all the places I've never been to, and all the places I've been to and want to revisit. I want to go to South America and see Rio, I'd love to tour the West Indies, I've got the feeling that if I went to Hawaii I might never come back. The thought of visiting Japan fascinates me and Ceylon is an exotic mystery I would love to investigate. I have not been to any of those places and would like to do so. And what about the places I've been to and want to revisit. I'd like once more to see the sun set on Jerusalem, April in Paris, autumn in New York, any time in San Francisco and Dublin when its raining and I feel like getting drunk and listening to good talk.

So my perfect trip would be a discovery of new wonders and also old joys revisited. And as it is to be the last trip I shall ever make it has one further virtue: it will last a long time. With any amount of luck and skilful planning it might even last foreever. And that would be the perfect holiday.

CLIFF MICHELMORE

> *Forget six counties overhung with smoke,*
> *Forget the snorting steam and piston stroke,*
> *Forget the spreading of the hideous town*
> *And dream of London, small and white and clean.*
>
> —William Morris

THAT did it. I know my dream holiday. Not for me the wine dark sea, burning sands and browning bodies, the counting of calories and minks. I shall dream.

By noon on Friday next, all vehicles (except bicycles) will be removed from the precincts of London and taken at least forty miles from Charing Cross and are not to return until noon the following Monday. All aircraft are forbidden to fly within sixty miles of the aforesaid Charing Cross and no chimney has permission to smoke within the same area. There shall be no television or radio transmissions nor shall there be any newspapers, magazines or other such matter published. No cinema shall show any film other than one having a U certificate. All employees of and owners of joints, strip, gambling, clip, bingo etc. to take the weekend off.

All public buildings, including Royal palaces, Government offices to be open to the public free of charge, and at all times throughout the weekend. It is the intention of my dream Government to allow families to see London as it should be, to take a long parting glance at it before the whole lot goes up in blocks, to walk the streets without fear of being knocked senseless by senseless drivers, and to breathe air without fear of being choked to death.

That is my dream holiday, with the family, just drifting around London. I have no great love of London, in truth I find it as comfortable and warming as a damp overcoat, but this weekend of standing and staring and drifting may just halt our idiot rush to nowhere.

And back to the dream for a moment. We have already booked Sir John Betjeman as our guide and companion for the weekend—so hands off !

Basil Boothroyd

I KNOW the place. The maddening thing is that I can't remember who told me about it, and I've forgotten where he said it was. It wasn't the place so much, anyway, but the hotel in it, and that's quite clear in my mind from what he told me. When you get there, it seems, after an aggregate airport delay of six hours, Reception behaves as if you're the one person it wanted to see, and knows you by name, instead of that air of My God here's another one and not having any trace of your booking. You are escorted swiftly to your room by a man who knows you've paid your service and taxes in advance, and doesn't hang around with his hand out rushing you into swingeing miscalculations in the local currency. The room has the promised balcony overlooking the sea, not the usual stuck window facing on to a main coast road. Hot water comes out of the hot tap, instead of warm and rust-coloured out of both, and gentlemen don't have to hold the loo seat up with one hand. On excursions to see the Hittite Pudding Stones, or the tomb of Theobald the Stiff your six o'clock call comes at six o'clock, with breakfast, rather than not at all with no breakfast (meaning the last seat on the bus, over the wheels and with a broken arm-rest, and everybody thinking it's your bloody fault they're an hour late starting). There are no bookies from Bolton, or ladies who sit next to you in the sun telling a friend how they regularly take their teeth out at home, and not being able to is spoiling their holiday. The band is actual musical instruments, not banks of amplification that look like a Boeing control-panel and come right up through the legs of your bed. There aren't any gala dinners with all prices doubled. Or long, long waits for the last day's car to the airport that doesn't come, while you know anyway that you've been taken for another kind of ride, and that if you write the letter to the manager you've been composing all week he won't answer it.

Where *was* that place? Or was he just putting me on?

What Do You Mean, Splendide?

A hotel survival course by KEITH WATERHOUSE

Q. Perhaps I am highly-strung or something, but every time I stay in a hotel I think I am about to have a nervous breakdown. This feeling is brought on by indifferent service, inefficient management and always being put over the ballroom. Should I hang myself instead of going on holiday this year?

A. *You do not say whether you are working to a budget. If expense is no object, why not take me along with you and book me into the next room when my advice will be available at all reasonable hours?*

Q. Thank you. Here we are at the hotel, then, and as you have just heard with your own ears, my first problem is that they are full to the rafters and deny all knowledge of my advance booking.

A. *Luckily for us you have about your person a letter from the management, confirming the booking.*

Q. Actually, I haven't. It never arrived.

A. *Then for God's sake look as if it did arrive and stop sliding around the reception desk as if you were trying to get a room for Mr. and Mrs. Smith. Tell the manager that you are not interested in the problems he has been having with temporary personnel. Tell him that you would sooner slit your throat than stay in the alternative accommodation he suggests. Tell him the reason you refuse to produce the letter confirming the booking is that you may need it in evidence. All this will get you a reputation as a troublemaker, and we will be given our rooms.*

Q. Here I am in my room but it does not have a bath, although I specified one in my booking.

A. *Have you allowed the porter to dump your suitcase on a sort of large camp-stool with a canvas slatted top?*

Q. Yes.

A. *Did you tip him?*

Q. Yes. Two shillings. (Ten new pence.)

A. *Then I am afraid that you have had it. You are welcome to have a bath in my room directly. Why my room has a bath and yours hasn't is that I refused point-blank to take possession of one lacking that elementary convenience. For that reason, you will find me in the bridal suite.*

Q. Now we are in the Louis Quatorze Grill-room on the mezzanine, and they are refusing to give us anything to eat on the grounds that it is after 6.45 pm. Must we go hungry?

A. *No. Quote the Innkeeper's Liability Act.*

Q. But surely that is to do with lost luggage and so forth?

A. *The Cypriot head waiter is not to know that. Just quote it. You may also tell him, in case he is thinking of doing anything unspeakable to the soup before wheeling it in, that I am the chief inspector of* The Good Food Guide.

Q. We are having a few post-prandial brandies together in the resident's lounge and I am finding it increasingly difficult to attract the night porter's attention. Why is this?

A. *This is because the night porter, like all night porters, is a puritan who thinks our monstrous licensing laws should not allow of any loophole for hotel residents. He will not bring us any more brandy until you make it clear that there will be an ugly scene otherwise.*

Q. Here he comes now. Perhaps you could pay, since I have run out of money and it is your round.

A. *Sign the bill.*

Q. But the night porter says I may not sign the bill.

A. *Give the night porter five shillings (twenty-five new pence) and ask him if you may borrow his pen. By the way, you might as well make those doubles while you are about it.*

Q. Now I am up in my room and it is 2.15 am.

A. *Yes, I see it is. I did specify, you know, that my advice was available at all* reasonable *hours.*

Q. I know, and that is the very point I want to take up. There is a sort of cardboard pyramid on my dressing-table with the printed information that room service operates for twenty-four hours. I want a cheese sandwich.

A. *If you think I am going to make it for you, you must be insane.*

Q. No, not you, *them.* I got through to the switchboard, after a delay of ten minutes, and they said they would ring me back. That was half an hour ago. How long must I wait?

A. *For ever, if you are going to swallow that particular ploy. Ring the switchboard again and tell them —*

Q. That I want the night waiter immediately?

A. *Clearly you have not stayed in many hotels, or you would know*

"Great news, your Majesty, the attempted revolution has been crushed."

that the night waiter is supposed to be off with 'flu. Ring the switch-board and dictate the following telegram to the chairman of the group controlling this hotel. DEAR HENRY YOU LOSE YOUR BET STOP WAS REFUSED CHEESE SANDWICH AT TWO FIFTEEN ACK EMMA REGARDS. *You then await results, which should take five minutes.*

Q. The manager of the hotel is at my door with a cheese sandwich garnished with watercress. Should I tip him?

A. *No go to sleep.*

Q. I am sorry to disturb you again, but it is now breakfast-time. I have ordered fresh lemon juice—

A. *Fresh* lemon *juice? At this hour?*

Q. Yes, I am on a diet. Anyway, the waiter has just brought me tinned lemon juice. I have told him that it is tinned lemon juice but he swears that he has just squeezed the lemon himself. I can hardly call him a liar, can I?

A. *Is it the same fellow we had the barney with about dinner last night?*

Q. Yes. The one who said he would swing for you.

A. *What you do then is this. Produce a test tube from your pocket. Pour the lemon juice carefully into it, cork it, and make an inscrutable entry in a small black notebook. The fresh lemon juice will be brought to you personally by the chef, together with an explanation of there having been ze mistake in ze kitchen.*

Q. While packing, I have found another sort of cardboard pyramid which says the management regrets that bills cannot be settled by cheque. Owing to your having drunk all that brandy last night, I have not the cash to meet my commitments. Should we get out through the window?

A. *Certainly not. Send a little note to the management regretting that bills cannot be settled in cash. You will then pay by cheque and ask them what they propose to do about it.*

Q. One final question. I am being asked for fifteen per cent service charge. Should I tip the man who whistles up our cab?

A. *Of course not, have this one on me. I say, can you lend me a bob (five new pence)?*

"They certainly don't look bankrupt to me!"

How it
all Started

Lady (to Messrs. Cook's official). "I HAVE NOTHING TO DECLARE. WHAT SHALL I SAY?"
Official. "SAY, MADAM, THAT YOU HAVE NOTHING TO DECLARE."
Lady. "YES; BUT SUPPOSE THEY FIND SOMETHING?"

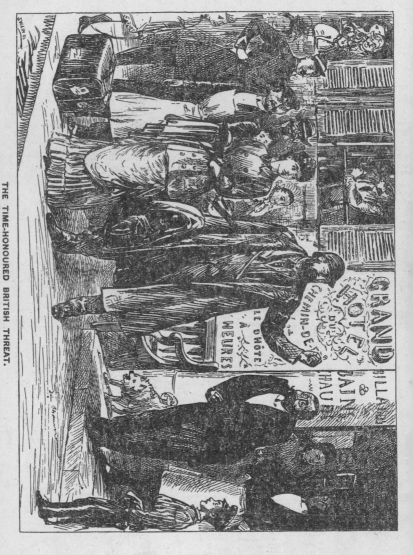

THE TIME-HONOURED BRITISH THREAT.

Indignant Anglo-Saxon (to Provincial French Innkeeper, who is bowing his thanks for the final settlement of his exorbitant and much-disputed account), "OH, OUI, MOSSOO! POUR LE MATTRAS DE ÇA, JE PAYE! MAIS JUSTE VOUS REGARDEZ ICI, MON AMI! ET JUSTE—VOUS—MARQUEZ—MES—MOTS! JE PAYE—MAIS JE METTS LE DANS LA 'TIMES'!"

'Arry has purchased a "Round Tour" (Hotel coupons included) to the Italian Lakes, Venice, &c., and has got to know, en route, a wealthy American momma and her daughters. At breakfast he's friends indulge largely in jam. 'Arry promptly orders some.

Head Waiter. "Is Monsieur aware that Jam is an extra?"

SCENE—*The Summit of Vesuvius.*

American Tourist (to the world at large). "GREAT SNAKES, IT REMINDS ME OF HELL!"
English Tourist. "MY DEAR, HOW THESE AMERICANS DO TRAVEL!"

Friend (to female with enormous pile of luggage). "HALLO, DEAR! WHERE ARE YOU SPENDING THE WEEK-END?"

IN SEARCH OF SUNSHINE.

"So this is Algiers!"

OUR COUNTRYMEN ABROAD.

Sketch of a Bench on the Boulevards, occupied by Four English People who only Know each Other by Sight.

THE MAN WHO HAD SEEN EVEREST.

Most obliging Guide (*brightly*). "PLEASE KEEP YOUR SEATS. THE DRIVER AND I ARE JUST GOING TO PICK YOU A FEW ALPINE ROSES."

COLD COMFORT.

Visitor to the West Indies (who has been warned against bathing in the river because of alligators, but has been told by the boatman that there are none at the river's mouth). "By Jove, this is ripping! But, I say, how do you know there are no alligators here?"

Boatman. "Well, you see, sah, de alligator am so turr'ble feared ob de shark!"

"ASTONISHING THE NATIVES."

First Alpine Tourist. "I SAY, WILL, ARE YOU ASLEEP?" *Second Tourist.* "ASLEEP? NO, I SHOULD THINK NOT! HANG IT, HOW THEY BITE!" *First Tourist.* "TRY MY DODGE. LIGHT YOUR PIPE, AND BLOW A CLOUD UNDER THE CLOTHES! THEY LET GO DIRECTLY. THERE'S A LOT PERCHED ON THE FOOT-RAIL OF MY BED NOW—COUGHING LIKE MAD!"

WE SHOULD HAVE ENJOYED OUR TRIP ABROAD
IMMENSELY—

IF WE HADN'T KNOWN THAT AUNT
SOPHIA WOULD EXPECT SOME SLIGHT
SOUVENIR ON OUR RETURN—

THAT UNCLE JOHN WOULD LOOK
FOR SOME LITTLE REMEMBRANCE—

THAT COUSIN AGATHA WOULD
BE MUCH HURT IF SHE WAS
OVERLOOKED—

AND SO WOULD HORACE AND
LITTLE AGAMEMNON AND BABY
AND NURSE—

AND COOK AND ALL THE MAIDS
AND THE GARDENER'S BOY—

AND THE MEMBERS OF THE
WOMEN'S GUILD AND THE
VILLAGE BOYS' CLUB—

AND THE ALMSHOUSES—

AND THE SUNDAY-SCHOOL.

OF COURSE NEXT TIME WE REALLY MUST TAKE THEM ALL
WITH US, AND THEN PERHAPS WE MIGHT GET A LITTLE
TIME TO SEE SOME OF THE SIGHTS WE CAME OVER FOR.

How They Brought the Staff from London to Boulogne

MILES KINGTON reads the minutes of the
Punch works outing to France

I'VE been working it out on a piece of graph paper left over from schooldays and there definitely is a pattern to *Punch* staff outings under the present regime. The first, in 1971, was a modest boat trip a few miles up the Thames. The next was a coach trip to Margate. Then came the grand outing to Newmarket races. And now, or rather last Tuesday, we spent a day in train, bus and Boulogne. It's what they call a geometric progression, and, if my graph is correctly drawn, 1979 should be the year of the first round-the-world *Punch* day outing. But wherever the editor's dreams take us in future, there will always be some constants, some unchanging features which will enable you to recognise a *Punch* excurison if you see it. There will be about thirty people with nothing conceivable in common. They will always be the last passengers to walk up the gangway or mount the train, and miraculously the first to arrive at the bar. They will split up into small groups—cartoonists to discuss money, writers to discuss the next round, and Alan Coren being guided by friends till he gets used to his sun glasses. And running from group to group, chasing the source of laughter, will be a worried individual with a notebook and pencil. This is the man who has been elected to write up the chronicle of the whole expedition.

My first note says "Robert Morley's swimming trunks". I wonder what that means. I know I planned to make a note of what people are wearing, but I distinctly remember Robert Morley in a purple shirt . . . It's beginning to come back now. 8.30 am, Victoria Station. Robert and Sheridan Morley, the first father-and-son act on a *Punch* outing. They have both brought swimming equipment.

"The pool at Boulogne is *marvellous,*" says father. "The French really know how to organise the seaside. That's why we joined the Common Market, you know. We found out too late about their towns."

At 8.45 the Folkestone train leaves, the bar opens and Richard Gordon starts the *Times* crossword. He fills in four clues on the run and sits back stunned. Ann Leslie sneezes, produces a vast packet of anti-streaming-nose pills and looks helplessly at Richard Gordon. Did he not, after all, write *Doctor at Sea* and many others?

"You may consult me on the boat," he says. "The one ailment I can treat with complete confidence is sea-sickness."

Really? What is the treatment?

"The treatment is to leave the patient completely alone."

He starts reading the list of ingredients on Ann Leslie's cold-pill package, and deduces that although they will be of little help in stemming her nose, they should be surprisingly good at stopping sea-sickness.

"I'm very good on sea-sickness."

At 9.30 Michael Heath prescribes a tin of lager for himself and becomes the first to take to drink. Michael Heath is generally reckoned a snappy dresser and is indeed the only *Punch* cartoonist who is greeted by wolf whistles when delivering his drawings at the office. But today, under interrogation, he feels he has come second-best to Barry Humphries, the amazing Australian, who is wearing a monocle, a white suit, a Panama hat, a billowing, maroon bow-tie, a red check shirt, brown and white shoes and a yellow handkerchief.

"I like it," says Mike Heath through gritted teeth.

"Something to start the day off with," says Barry Humphries lightly. "I have several changes of clothing with me."

Michael Heath vanishes to get another lager. By the time he re-appears we are backing down Folkestone quay alongside the *Horsa*, pride of the British Rail Sealink navy. After the short ceremony in Customs of jeering at Stanley Reynolds, standing lonely with his American passport in a queue by himself, we take our place behind the 700 people going up the gangway and reappear first at the bar. Not so Robert Morley though, who has gone on deck to supervise departure and is already surrounded by autograph hunters. Sheridan Morley stands to one side (he already has his father's autograph) and explains the process.

"The same thing always happens when people recognise my father. They know his face but can't remember the name. They go up to him and say, 'It's . . . it's . . .'. He says, 'Robert Morley?' They say, 'Right!' Then they say, 'It's not for me, it's for my daughter'."

A schoolgirl goes mad with success and asks William Davis for his autograph. He signs, and puts underneath 'EDITOR OF PUNCH'.

"Know what that is?"

"A comic," she says.

Fair enough. Just as I am repeating this little episode to a colleague, I notice a lady writing it down in her notebook. It is attractive Valerie Jenkins who is reporting the trip for the *Evening Standard* and has the nerve to steal *my* material. Tempers flare, there is a brief scuffle and I am held fast in the attractive iron grip of Valerie Jenkins.

"Have a heart," she says, twisting my wrist a bit further. "I'm phoning the piece in at two, and I need material more than you do."

We do a deal. She agrees to cover the remarks made by Robert Morley to the captain ("Where do you log your mutinies?") and I agree to report what the captain says to Robert Morley ("Would you mind letting me have your autograph? It's not for me, it's for my daughter.") But I hold out on her about Richard Gordon. She thinks he is just standing on deck. I don't tell her that at this very moment he is treating everyone on the ship for sea-sickness.

After an uneventful crossing—i.e. we reach France without hitting another ship—the fair city of Boulogne emerges from the sunny mist and we slide into the harbour of the town we have come so far to see. There are gay waterside buildings with gay signs like "Watney Red Barrel" and "Under English Ownership" and "Chips". As we leave the ship, we find two brand-new, apparently abandoned Leyland lorries.

"There it is!" cries Alan Coren. "It's Britain's trade deficit, lying rusting on the foreshore at Boulogne! Someone in Whitehall ought to know about this," He spots me scribbling in my little book and grasps the bruises left by Valerie Jenkins. "Watch it, Kington. It's too early in the day to start taking a man's conversation down."

We are whisked by bus to a reception in the Chambre de Commerce, a gay waterfront building with a fine view of the *Horsa*, pride of the Sealink navy.

"Strange," muses Alan Coren to himself, or so he thinks. "Never knew they got ink from seals." He spots me scribbling, snaps his sun glasses across his face and moves away. There is a general move towards a counter holding lovely cool champagne, but the barman shakes his head and says: "Non, non, pas encore. Après le discours." *Discours?* Ah yes, the speech of welcome by the vice-president of the Chambre de Commerce who, I am delighted to see later, is mistakenly described in the *Evening Standard* by a certain Valerie Jenkins as the deputy mayor of Boulogne. He presents a sailor's hat and a bag of mussels to William Davis, who makes a graceful reply in absolutely faultless English and looks fab in the hat. Discours over, the company edges towards the champagne and is besieged by the local press and radio. When was *Punch* founded? Is there anything like it in France? What on earth are you doing in Boulogne? Richard Gordon is seen talking fluent French into a *France Inter* microphone. I believe he is telling French listeners how to deal with sea-sickness. Robert Morley is asked his opinion of Boulogne. "It's very English. I mean that as a compliment, of course. I think perhaps the general question of air-conditioning could be gone into more closely, but poor things, they've been taken by surprise by our English summer coming over and they're not ready for it."

Then back into the bus and off to lunch at 2 pm. Hotel Marmin, Place Monsigny. An upstairs room. Pâté with port jelly (très bien). Sole en champagne (mmm). Aiguillette de canard (translated by Basil Boothroyd as "Canadian eagle" and very good). Cheese (I can recommend the bleu d'Auvergne). Crêpes suzette (ouf !). Muscadet, very good claret, champagne, calvados. What more can one say? The answer, of course, is that I can tell you the brilliant conversation that flies around the table, and here I must confess to failure. Not a single note remains from lunch, a pithy remark reading "Basil almost choked to death".

What that means is this. Over the crêpes suzette Barry Took suddenly bursts into a classic, never-to-be-forgetton imitation of Maurice Chevalier singing, winking, ogling, charming his way through a five-minute monologue until everyone is crying with laughter except Basil Boothroyd who is choking to death. When he recovers he says to me: "I'm sorry for you. All you can do to describe that, is write 'Barry Took was very funny for five minutes'. What else can you say?"

"Well," I say, "I can write 'Basil Boothroyd almost choked to death'."

Robert Morley actually knows a story about Boulogne, though.

"Two well-known, romantic British journalists, —— and ——, came here for the day and found that they had a peculiar taste in common. They liked being flagellated. So they made inquiries about the whereabouts of a certain establishment and were recommended to a house in the town. There they went, and explained to the madame what their requirements were. She drew herself up to her full height and said sternly: 'Messieurs, c'est une maison *sérieuse*!'."

Lunch ends at 4.15 and we have only an hour before sailing in which to see Boulogne. It is then that I discover that behind the English quarter there is a perfectly good and nice French town, where I stroll contentedly until embarkation. That is not true, of course. I dash frantically from shop to shop, getting pâté, French bread, bonbons pour les enfants, croissants for breakfast tomorrow, a little something for the wife and keepsakes for my other forty-nine relatives. I also find a restaurant with a bilingual menu which puzzles me. Every French item is faithfully translated into English except "Assiette Anglaise" for which the English is "Assiette Anglaise." What can it be?

We reassemble in the bus and wait half an hour for Alan Coren, who does not turn up.

"Where the hell is the Deputy Editor?" laughs William Davis.

"I think he is avoiding me," I suggest, but he does not believe me. We give him up for lost and make the boat with five minutes to spare. It is a very nice French boat with many pleasant features including the well-known Alan Coren in the bar, where he has been sitting worrying about us. There is also a restaurant which serves Assiette Anglaise, translated as "chicken and other cold meats". I think this is a French insult.

To while away the uneventful crossing to Folkestone, I now

"Sunshine or not I'll be damned glad when this observation stint's over and we can get back to Mars."

conduct a ruthless survey of what everyone has bought on their trip to the Common Market. Strangely, at least half our travellers have bought nothing beside refreshment, but there are some revealing purchases.

David Langdon: "I bought a string of garlic, reckoning it would be cheaper from a shop than from a bicycle in England. Actually, I'm not sure how much it was. I gave him £25 and accepted the change."

William Davis: "Three kinds of sausage."

Barry Humphries: "I was tempted by two vases in the Art Nouveau style—that's French for ugly—but they were £100 each. I also acquired some perfume by chafing myself vigorously against the ladies in the party."

Jeremy Kingston: "Half a kilo of greengages and two cowrie shells."

Victor Caudery, chairman of *Punch*: "If you really want to know, I had a lovely snooze at the hotel bar."

Paul Callan, *Daily Mail* diary editor: "J'ai acheté . . . une lanterne style rue de Carnaby . . . pour ma femme Americaine, Steffi . . . ca s'écrit S-T-E-F-F-I."

Sheridan Morley: "I'm glad you asked me that question. I have bought a kit for making your own stained-glass windows. You don't believe me, do you? Look."

And it is. But where is Robert Morley?

"Ah. This may sound strange, but my father is very fond of a little gambling, and when we heard that one of our hosts was driving to Le Touquet tonight, he remembered that he had never been to the casino there and decided to stay for a few more days. He should be all right. He's got all my francs."

Richard Gordon is asleep.

At Folkestone we all leave the boat, jeer at Stanley Reynolds in the queue for Americans and board our train, an English one. The bar is closed ("Police orders, sir—had an awful lot of trouble") and soon the search is on for a corkscrew to break into duty-free wines. I have a corkscrew on my penknife and am temporarily the most popular man on board.

Stanley Reynolds is asleep.

Paul Callan is sitting opposite Alan Hall, editor of the *Sunday Times*'s Atticus column. Have you ever seen two top diary editors take each other's shoes and socks off, and write insults on each other's feet? I have. They probably won't mention this in their columns.

Several shipboard romances threaten to flare up, but are easily beaten off by our lady guests, hardened in the battlefield of Fleet Street.

I am asleep.

At Victoria we all wake up, pile into taxis and race each other to Hyde Park Corner, having agreed that the food was good, the wine bracing and the sea air very good vintage. I gain an exclusive interview with Alan Coren just before leaving, anxious to trap him into agreeing to comment on the trip.

Alan Coren (lowering his voice): "Very nice, really. But don't quote me on that."

"Has phar la houdla seel vo plate?"

"Glhup hwow you shoul do da?"

111

WILLIAM HARDCASTLE:

PINK AS
THE ACE OF SPADES

We started black near the Equator and became pinker and paler as we moved north. Something to do with letting the Vitamin D in through our skins. The process took several million years but the end result is all those beautiful blondes in Iceland. I speak with the authority of Professor Jacob Bronowski, who's not the sort of chap I choose to argue with. But what he has not explained to my satisfaction is why, having gone to all this trouble, we are so fond of turning ourselves black again, or as near to it as a suntan can achieve.

Suntan is a cult, a success symbol, an industry that fills hundreds of jet planes and thousands of hotel rooms each week. It also controls a separate and very successful segment of the cosmetic industry, as a glance at all those bottles of goo on the chemists' shelves will tell you. Personally I think it's a lot of tosh, but that's perhaps because I was born only slightly south of the Arctic Circle, viz., Newcastle-on-Tyne.

The sun doesn't carry a lot of tanning-potential up there. When I was a child I knew it was summer because the daylight was longer. We used to get *wind* burn and rosy cheeks were a natural by-product of the north-easters that started in Lapland, funnelled down the Norwegian fjords and came to us via the North Sea.

We were ready for them on the beaches. Childhood photographs of the author on the Northumberland Riviera show a lad dressed as if for cod-fishing off the Faroes. Oh, yes, we bathed and we always knew when it was time to come out; our lips went blue. Then it was a dash up the sand to the windbreak we had staked out in the dunes, a thermos of tea and a couple of ginger biscuits.

I suppose I did meet people with suntans but I ignored them as unreliable and probably foreign types, gigolos with a tendency to tango, and we all knew what *that* meant. There were occasions when the sun came out and it was hot for several days, but the nearest I got to a tan was shocking pink. I had the quickest-peeling nose for miles around. I enjoyed myself but that was unaware of the pleasures lying rump to buttock on a racky Latin strand and being spit-roasted by the Mediterranean sun while the scent of a hundred different lotions—a sort of human barbecue—assailed the nostrils.

Nowadays, of course, I realise that suntans are essential. There is no deeper shame than coming back from a holiday *pale*. Not all the comic bullfight posters, funny sombreros, or chug-a-lugging wine flasks will compensate for a skin that has not been fried to the shade of a strong cup of tea, or, at the very least, milky instant coffee. Consider, therefore, my personal plight—I don't *like* getting tanned.

This may be accounted for by the distance of my birthplace from the Equator and the hospitality my pores show to Vitamin D. There is also a scarcity of hair on the top of my head. This makes me vulnerable to a *coup de soleil* on a grey day in Wigan. It also drains my sparse foreign currency reserves. Normally I never wear any headgear but I have the damnest collection of Andalusian berets, Panama hats and Arabian fezzes purchased at high cost in distant parts. But it's not my cranium I worry about most—it's my feet.

Picture me on a fashionable lido, striking, though I say it as shouldn't, quite a figure. All I'm wearing are a flattering pair of trunks and a canvas hat from which the motto "Kiss Me Quick" has been judiciously removed. The rest of me has been annointed with sun-tan oil at the rough cost of 1000 lire per square inch of epidermis. *But I've forgotten the top of my feet.* Normally my feet

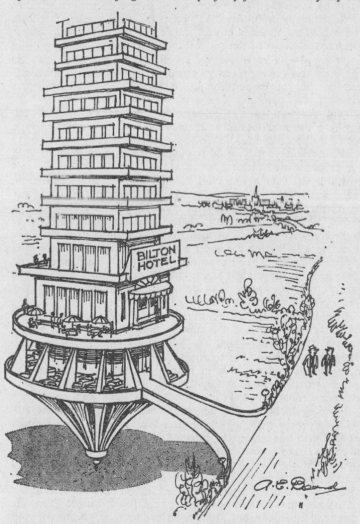

"That?—oh, remember that stunt somebody got up to a while back of selling Americans a foot of English soil for ten dollars?"

tops are reminiscent of a snake's belly—pale and interesting—but only a few minutes of Mediterranean sun and they can become like two small and extremely painful Tahitian sunsets. Which results in shaming conversations like this:

Have a good holiday?
No.
You're not very brown.
No.
Bad weather?
No, I burnt my feet.

I'm surprised that nobody has thought of marketing foot-shades. I'm sure I'm not the only sufferer and modern technology has already developed many useful devices to offset the more unpleasant effects of sun-bathing. You can buy plastic covers for your nose so that it doesn't race ahead of the rest of your face and turn deep purple. There are also those whose lips are allergic to excessive sunshine. For them there is a protective cream, and what does it matter if they look like they're auditioning for the Black and White Minstrel Show?

I will grant you that I'm jealous of those who tan easily and well. But have you ever looked at them when their tan begins to fade (which is as soon as they get on the aeroplane to take them home)? Within a few days they could be taken for a case of jaundice. And that tanned torso? After a bit it will just look as if they haven't washed lately. They have a mark round the middle like a used bath.

The word "tan" is short for tanning which, according to my encyclopaedia, is "the process of converting hides and skins into leather". Well said, Britannica, There are those who burn themselves to the colour consistency of their boy friend's brief case, and look attractive with it. But, for sheer magnetism give me the pale lady who sits in the shade of a tree twirling her parasol. What the cosmetic advertisements suggest will be a sexy tan too often turns out to be the leathery look. Personally I like women to have a slightly softer consistency than a pair of well-worn motoring gloves.

A few years ago there were attempts to bring the chemical arts of the leather industry into the sun-tan business. You could get an Acapulco appearance, went the advertising copy, without going further than Balham. The treatment was roughly the equivalent of marinating the human body in prune juice, turning regularly. The snag was that you could end up streaky, and I knew a poor girl who had to go around for weeks insisting that no, she hadn't got leprosy.

Browning the body is, in fact, very much a twentieth-century cult and didn't really take hold until after World War I. Prior to that, bronzed flesh was largley the mark of the labouring classes who had no choice but to expose themselves to the elements. It is curious that a round-the-year tan has now become the badge of well-heeled indolence. But the irony does give me hope, that while my opinion is not widely shared at present, the wheel of fashion could turn again.

Do you wish to look like an English rose? Well, come to Cornwall. Its rainfall exceeds that of Manchester and nothing is better for your complexion. Don't dry your skin up in Portofino or Las Palmas. Let British rainwater work its magic—and think of the money you'll save on suntan oil and dark spectacles!

114

Not the Only Pebble on the Beach

VINCENT MULCHRONE v. the Madding Crowd

FUNNY how you go off people. I've just gone off Charlie Chaplin and Oona. They've blown Evoia.

It's just a little Greek island, barely known as a tourist haunt. But that's where they're going for their holiday. And if the discerning Chaplins have chosen it, can the travel brochures for a dozen half-finished hotels be far behind?

For some years now, Evoia has been the secret place for a friend of mine who is a travel writer. He has a couple of other quiet places stashed away, so he's not entirely destitute. But Charlie Chaplin has cut his private discoveries by about a third.

Considering their privileged position—free trips, and grog, and all—our travel writers are a remarkably honest bunch in my experience. But they are human, too, And part of their job is to steer the masses where *they* are not. They don't actually cheat. They simply write in a private language, clear as a bookie's tic-tac to each other, but unnoticed by the general public churning through acres of holiday supplements in early January.

You have to know your travel writer, of course, and even the nuances. "Quiet resort" could well mean they roll up the pavements, supposing they have pavements, at 9 p.m. "Quietly positioned" can generally be taken to mean that it's miles away from anywhere and the bus comes most Tuesdays. "Centrally situated" is a danger signal, because your balcony could overlook the all-night disco. Fine if you happen to be a disco fan who has rumbled the code.

Before we leave wunnerful Greece, take a sentence in a travel article going something like this: "Take the ferry which plies regularly from Piraeus, calling in at dear old Poros, then on to the gaiety of Hydra and the unique charms of Milos."

Now, which of those three islands do you suppose the writer prefers? You're right. It's Poros. He had to mention it because he loves it and spends holidays there. Privately he wouldn't spend more than a quick lunchtime among the pseudo-transatlantic artists who have turned Hydra into a caricature.

I was in Lloret de Mar in 1949 when the only other Englishman in the village was the present Speaker of the House of Commons. He didn't speak. Neither did I.

But if he was thinking what I was thinking, it was that the other wouldn't be so stupid as to spread the news at home that there existed a rough and ready, fantastically cheap stretch of the Spanish coast called the Costa Brava. Anyway, *I* didn't snitch.

Neither, generally speaking, do the travel writers. Some do private swops. One, with a lien on a £100 cottage on the undiscovered Costa del Tuppence, can bank on a colleague holding off for a while. Otherwise he just *could* write a piece about the Anatolian bay where the other gets his ouzo for a penny, b. and b. for 50p, *and* change out of a quid for the whole day. It may not be an exclusively British trait, but it is a fact that, when it comes to holidays, the rich and the poor tend to stick together—that is, the rich with the rich, and the poor with the poor.

The rich go to the length of building stockades around their mini-villages in the West Indies. They may not know much about the West Indies, but at least a chap knows whose wife he's bathing with. Travel writers steer clear.

At the other end of the scale, among the package tours, they perform a valuable service if only in advising people not to book into an hotel which appears in the travel brochure as an "artist's impression."

Occasionally they slip up, like the rest of us. I once found myself in an hotel in Ibiza which was unfinished and practically unstaffed. Well recommended by several travel writers who hadn't been there, its lifts were still being installed. The only happy couple there were honeymooners who gladly ran up six flights of stairs. The putative foyer shook with the protests of the one-legged, middle-aged, Englishman who had long since lost the urge for speed but still wanted to get to his bed on the fourth floor without doing himself a damage.

The travel writers, as I say, have the advantage on most of us because they get there first, and want to hug their new-found joy to themselves for a little while.

(Well, perhaps not first. That distinction goes to the cabin crews of the big jets who, given a two or three day rest period—known as "slipping"—anywhere around the main routes, go off at a tangent and find gloriously cheap spots which they enjoy and then abandon at first sight of a batch of blue-rinsed matrons from Decatur, Ala.)

One wonders what travel writers for foreign papers say about us? ("That's a deal then, Hank. I lay off Ullswater, and you lay off the East Coast until I get my cottage in Cleethorpes tied up").

It must be the sheer speed with which they "do" Yurrup that makes so many Americans fall victim to the "If it's Tuesday it *must* be Naples" syndrome. Ask the men who run the Thames pleasure boats. They say that confusion between the Tower of London and the Leaning Tower of Pisa is commonplace. And they're tired of being asked "When do we pass Notre Dame?"

Where the travel writers do send them is to Fleet Street, where they pack into a hostelry called the Cheshire Cheese. There, on steamy August days, they tuck into the speciality of the house, steak and kidney pud. The sight is something of a tourist attraction in itself. I'd rate it a two-star eye-opener.

On behalf of these people—and tourism *is* our fourth biggest industry—there has been some pressure for *two* Changings of the Guard, even when the absence of the Royal Standard says she's not home. But the Army won't have it. And, as Lord Mancroft put it, "It's a palace—not the Palladium."

I believe my travel-writing chum when he says, "We know our class of readership, and try to steer them to the places that we feel would be right for them." And the power of their pens can be extraordinary.

"For God's sake, Gerald, unwind gradually!"

Some years ago, the doyenne of the trade wrote to the effect that the South coast of Turkey and the West coast of Ireland were the last unspoiled coastlines in Europe. Immediately both, tourist-wise, took off.

I could have cut her throat, because I had "discovered" West Cork and was keeping quiet about it. Not so an ex-journalist friend, now a famous Labour MP, who extolled its beauties in a national daily.

I met him walking along the shore with a face as long as P. J. O'Sullivan's bar. "Whassup?" sez I. Wassup was that dozens of readers were begging for the exact location. He fought them off for weeks, telling them that Cork was full of lovely bays, and they should pick their own. But one reader persisted until the MP and amateur travel writer committed the cardinal sin of the craft, He told the reader exactly *where*.

"And guess what?" said this broken man. "When I got up this morning, this bugger's pitched his tent right alongside my caravan. He says he's always wanted to meet me. And t'bugger's staying a *fortnight*."

There was nothing to say. We both turned for P. J. O'Sullivan's. It seemed the only way out.

Make Way for the Group!

E. S. TURNER does so, grumbling like crazy

"ARE you one of the group?" asks the head waiter. "No," you reply. He surveys his tables planted with little American flags and then, radiant with guilt offers you a small table beside the service doors. You point out that it is being used as a dump by waiters, but he says he can fix that.

"There is a group," he explains, as one would say, "There are locusts" or "There are sand-bugs." Last-night there was no group. Tomorrow there will be no group. But tonight there is a group.

We had already met the group, on the ferry to Tangier. They streamed aboard at Algeciras, one hundred and sixty-six members of a department store in Minnesota. Amiable and unabrasive people, but, like all groups, upsetting the law of averages wherever they went. (The other day a Moroccan ran amok on this ferry with a knife, perhaps not liking to see the law of averages mocked).

The very existence of the party from Minnesota spoke much for the esprit de corps of department stores in the Middle West. Who would have thought that haberdashery would elect to tour the casbahs with men's toiletries, or theatre booking share a room with costume jewellery? How was the store getting on without this sizable sales force?

On the hotel roof, beside the pool, the sales ladies talked shop. One of them let it be known that she was expected to run fifteen departments with only five telephones. There was general agreement that only by travelling the world could you really get to know the folk in the next department. Therein, perhaps, is the secret of the attraction of the group.

They took the usual movies in the souks. Perhaps the day will come when a couple of Moroccan groups turn up in that store in Minnesota to photograph the native women, in their picturesque curlers, buying vibrators and gadabout bags.

People who are worried about the environment ought to start worrying about groups. Already they threaten the quality of life. They are a major infestation on the Great Circle routes of the world. They jostle other forms of life almost to extinction. Wherever they descend they consume everything in sight, not only food and liquor but joke ashtrays and camel saddles. No one knows where they will strike next. One moment they are looting Taormina, the next they are sacking Stratford. They suborn all service and their baggage is always first up on the airport carrousels. They even get free drinks from mayors. (I am speaking of genuine groups, not ad hoc collections of bogus dahlia growers, who cohere only to get a cheap flight).

Groups can bring out latent paranoia in those who meet them. In Soviet Asia, a spacious enough land in all conscience, I was pursued by the same American group from Alma-Ata to Tashkent, from Tashkent to Samarkand. "Jeepers! You again!" they would exclaim, as they found me, in yet another people's republic, drinking champagne with meat balls (groups don't eat meat balls, they just leave them for others).

They deserted me to fly to Bokhara, while I went as a one-man group to Dushambe, but we met again in Moscow. They were still in vigorous form, with the wags of the party raising as many laughs as ever. In Moscow there were also East German groups, who were quiet and disciplined and had the knack of easing out champagne corks with only the tiniest hiss. They did not seem to eat meat balls, either.

I do not suppose I have been as much exposed to groups as, let us say, Mr J. Hart Rosdail, of Elmhurst, Illinois. The *Guinness Book of Records* nominates him as the most indefatigable globe-trotter, with 209 countries to his credit. Perhaps—a fearful thought—he visited them all as a member of a group. Naturally I prefer to think that he covered his million-odd miles as a loner; but nowadays there are countries, like Albania, which you can visit only if you join a group.

It is possible to be beset by groups, not only on land, sea and in the air, but under the earth. What do you find in the catacombs of the Early Christians on the Appian Way? Jammed into a 2000-year-old micro-chapel, an English ladies' bowling club waits while a herd of Bavarians jostle through the sacred vaults. As the sporting ladies try to stick their heads out, a party of Swedes moves up, plainly displeased to find the chapel occupied. Round the corner Irish pilgrims are colliding head-on with Spanish travel agents, French lawyers, Danish hoteliers. Above ground more groups are marking time against the notices which say "English," "French," "Dutch," "Czech" and so on.

It's not much fun when you're queueing at the gates of the Vatican to see the couriers edging in front of you to buy sixty tickets each. Some places give cut prices to groups, which doesn't make sense to the independent tourist; or they allow groups to sneak through the turnstiles out of opening hours, which also is an injustice, except that it lightens the lot of those of us who take the trouble to exclaim over Grecian vases in authorised hours.

The group can cost you money, unexpectedly. There you are, in a quiet, delightful, non-touristy restaurant which you have cleverly discovered, with an attentive waiter wafting away crumbs like mad. Then in sweeps a hungry but still euphoric battalion from beyond the Rockies and the waiter deserts you to drag some giggly matron to her feet and jive with her. Musicians may emerge to serenade the group, boys may dance with trays of drinks on their heads. Since you are privileged to watch these excesses, you will be invited to reward the performers.

I expect to be told that international tourism is irrevocably geared to the group. Who wants to keep a hotel open for the odd vagrant like me, cooking rich dishes which are never ordered, when he can get a firm booking for a hundred Swiss neurologists just like that? Well, it's a point of view, but I sometimes wonder about the economics of it all. It is an eerie experience to arrive in a resort and wander into a great luxury hotel with its acres of burnished floor apparently untrodden by human foot. The lounges and bars are empty, no staff are visible, but the lights are on and the clocks are ticking. Has the place been evacuated because of a bomb scare? If it is really in business, how can it hope to recoup its overheads? Next day you look in again and the shimmering floors are hidden under a wall-to-wall chaos of luggage. The reception desk looks like the Siege of Acre. That night the head waiter will be explaining to chance arrivals "Yesterday was no group. Tomorrow is no group. But today is a group." Truly, the way to travel is to arrive between groups, but how does one plan it?

It would be wrong to be wholly ungrateful to groups. If you arrive late at a quayside, or an airport, you're all right if they're still waiting for a group. They don't mind leaving one person behind, or even an English football team, but they rarely leave a hundred. Sometimes you can sweep painlessly through Customs by tagging on to a high-powered group.

I am reminded, too, of a night spent at a pull-up near Algeciras with a sign: "Motel: Restaurant: Bullring." The bullring was the smallest imaginable, seating possibly a hundred people. It lay below the bedroom window and one could have popped a cork into it. Unfortunately it was a slack night at the motel. Had a group come along I feel sure the management would have staged a "friendly" for us, dressing up the more able-bodied waiters as matadors and sending for a lively young bull to chase them round the ring. That's the trouble with groups—they're never there when you want them.

"We'd better report back to Colonel Ivanov for Instructions!"

'The trouble is my wife hates going abroad . . .

. . . my daughter likes to lie on a Mediterranean beach . . .

. . and my son likes to climb mountains n Switzerland

Me? I don't mind what I do . . .

. . . so long as I get away from the office."

"*My dear chap, of* **course** *it's overweight. Whoever travels on holiday* **without** *paying excess?*"

"*Oh, what a bore—don't tell me they've misrouted my luggage to Bangkok* **again**."

"We always travel light—send our man Rogers ahead by road with the luggage."

"Good old fashioned coach-hide for his Lordship —wouldn't be seen dead with all this rubbishy lightweight stuff."

Lead and I Follow, Follow

PETER PRESTON in the
the grip of the travel-
mongers

A FEW years ago, young and innocent, I had a harrowing experience. A big professional organisation for travel agents wondered if a reporter would like to cover their annual conference. The reporter was me. The conference was in Norway.

We heaved across the North Sea in early winter, kept sane by a bountiful bar and a whimsical agent who explained the clotted legality of his bargain trips to Australia. We waited for coaches. We shivered in chill bedrooms. We spent hours at dinner tables attending the eventual arrival of cold and minute portions of local delicacies. They—the travel agents—moaned pitifully among themselves. I—the reporter—watched fascinated, taking it all down in a little book. Here were the men who sold holidays griping about the sort of holidays they sold. Here were the English abroad, and distinctly doleful because they'd got pickled herring for breakfast again.

It's a revelation one recalls whenever one meets a travel writer. I meet them regularly—usually en route to the Rocky Mountains or Japan. Where are you off to next? Oh, only Yugoslavia—but right off the beaten track. And then, maybe, the nethermost Mediterranean coast of Turkey. I met one a couple of months back in Minneapolis. What was he going to do? Hire a car and drive slap across the American mid-West; he didn't think anybody had ever done it before.

And that, alas, is the point. People go on holiday once or twice a year. The travel column goes on fifty-two weeks a year. The moneyed travel writer—with fat contract from "Holiday Magazine"—has a round-the-world ticket and, to take a true for instance, four articles to produce. It doesn't precisely encourage detailed coverage of small pensions in southern Brittany of cheap ski-ing chalets on Austrian railway lines. In fact it encourages the precise opposite: the scoop bizarre. That chunk of Yugoslavia no one had written up before turned out—to take a second true example—to be rocky wasteland, without inhabitants or hotels or even views to speak of. Why had no one chronicled a mid-West car trek before? Because the mid-West is huge, flat and uninteresting, unless you like corn on the cob.

Thus the system, born out of boredom and initiative intermingled, favours the esoteric. Who, in the sacred name of colour supplements, can go to Benidorm year after year and look Lord Thomson in the eye? Sooner or later one has to get hooked on the myth of the glossy spreads: real solitude, real wildness, real distance, twentieth-century man shedding neuroses among the (Sunday paper approved) peasants of some forgotten land. I have done it all. I fell in love with Switzerland when, at eighteen, I first discovered the efficiency of its sanitary waterworks and bid France's black holes farewell; but since then I have eaten Shepherd's Pie in the State Resthouse, Takoradi, removed a quarter-inch screw from ravioli in Rawalpindi, tramped the sacred cities of Morocco. I have suffered for the grand delusion.

At any cost—this delusion runs—one must escape the common herd. But the common herd, regrettably, know what's good. A friend lent me her "wonderfully quiet" shack in the south of France. It was wonderfully quiet because it was two hundred (vertical) yards from the nearest track. Water came from a nearby spring: full of lizards. Sanitation came from the nearby bushes: spiky. Wildlife burgeoned all around: rats. Forty-eight hours later, deeply grateful but infinitely wiser, we departed for a hotel in Antibes.

Even a little nearer civilisation the magnet of total normality still tugs. In a Moroccan cafe one must scrabble for fish and chips, the only dish the children eat. In a tiny Portuguese village one must hunt for tomato sauce. There is always—shamefaced and surreptitious—the long, long trail in search of an English newspaper and the glum certainty it will be a *Daily Telegraph*.

But surely—you say—somebody must relish solitude? Somebody, certainly: but damned elusive. Where do the army colonels and civil servants who superintended a distant Empire decamp to when their toil is done? To Cyprus (for example): attending the English Church in Kyrenia, drinking at the English pub in a Greek quarter back-street, buying frozen kippers, commuting in Mini-Mokes, forming bridge circles. What did the lone Lord I met in a beach cafe in Morocco or the lonely lady in caravan on the Costa Del Sol intend? Living off British tourists. What do roving foreign correspondents do as they patrol the globe? Meet in a few distant yet notorious bars and swap Fleet Street gossip.

The desolate trails, in short, are unloved and unlovable. They are enthusiastically populated only by those writers who find profes-sional cachet in desolation. They do, however, create a climate. They make the mundane a social burden; they make romantic adventure mandatory for post-humorous cocktail chat. And they have one substantial, mostly unacknowledged, sociological trait working for them: holiday horrors.

On that Norwegian trip the travel agents bitched constantly, but this didn't mean they weren't enjoying themselves. Everybody, tottering ashore at Newcastle, professed complete pleasure and meant it. The agonies had been part of the ecstasy. Man, returning to his lair, needed a smattering of ghoulish details to spice the colour slides with. Since holidays are mainly anticipation and retrospection, there's nothing more tedious for the remaining eleven months than bland comfort, perfect arrangements and unadulterated sun during the handful of weeks overseas. Every news editor knows that tales of British holidaymakers camping on a building site in Majorca (because their hotel won't be finished until next spring) make riveting copy. Readers identify with such plights. Readers want to feel that holidays can still be an adventure reserved for the brave.

Friends and neighbours, without supporting evidence, must be impressed by sagas of fortitude in faraway adversity.

Which is, unhappily, the reason why the long-distance master of purple prose will continue to wax and grow plump. Fewer travel agencies are collapsing in spectacular fashion. Fewer scandals are besetting Spanish tourism. Truly to suffer these days you have to cut adrift: alone in a very foreign land with all amenities as distant and intractable as possible. My richest aquaintance, having had a spot of bother in a flat-bottomed boat up the Amazon last year, is thinking of doing it again for want of anything more horrendous. My poorer aquaintances are vastly impressed with Albania's disaster potential. Meanwhile anyone seeking absolute quietude without tears might take a personal tip no travel writer would ever give: one of a dozen small Normandy resorts possessing splendid food, comfortable beds and complete peace. You need merely go in November (the month the travel writers recommended Tahiti).

Something New Under the Sun

BASIL BOOTHROYD tours the sun-drenched brochures

IF I tell you I'm just back from a holiday tour of nineteenth century slate mines you won't believe me, and you'll be right. But if you don't believe there are such things you'll be wrong What I've just drawn to your attention, through a fine cloud of nineteenth century slate dust, has just won an award from the British Tourist Authority—and that strong competition in the new ideas field from, and I tell you no lie, organ connoisseurs Baching around Germany, railway buffs studying the iron horses of Portugal, and Jersey market gardeners vacationing in Israel to see how the other half packs tomatoes.

Runners-up included those now rather drearified cooking, painting, slimming and Yoga hols, earlier attempts by the travel industry to stimulate the adventure buds of those sick of an oil-smeared period of semi-consciousness with Agatha Christie asleep on their chests.

Most of this isn't as new as you might think. I've had a yellowed *Sunday Times* clipping up my sleeve for a year or two:

"Intelligent, creative, fun-loving people, artists, writers, intellectuals, invited to join large group similar on Mediterranean Island . . ."

Admittedly, it seems to have been a one-off, and I haven't seen a repeat, greedily though I've combed the small ads for something equally tempting. I was strongly tempted by that one, in fact: tempted to find out which island and steer clear of it by a thousand nautical miles minimum. Perhaps you can't imagine parting a clump of bougainvillaea and running slap into this lot, standing around being intelligent and creative about whether Bishop Berkeley was the spiritual father of Spinoza, why *The Dynasts* has never been done into a ballet, and wondering if the tall blonde with the fun sunglasses would like to hear more behind a handy dune.

If, that is, any of the artists, writers, intellectuals and similar ever showed up. I'd guess not. So all the tall blonde and similar would get, after coming all the way from Ipswich with her autograph album and some questions she'd always wanted to ask Kenneth Clark about picture-framing, is a couple of unpublished poets and a man who once walked down a street in Ossett behind Stan Barstow.

I suppose that's why it never caught on. Or it may have been a mistake to throw in "fun-loving" in a largely cultural context. You want your clients to feel they're getting the best of two worlds, of course, if not more. But combine a Gastronome's Fortnight with Live With the Bedouins, Sheep's Eyes Optional, and they don't know where they are.

The sing-dance-and-rave-all-night customer, as I was hinting recently in these columns or similar, prefers sticking to that. Shove in a coach trip to a set of culverts, thought to prove that Agamemnon's uncle was a plumber, and you've put them off the Peloponnese for good.

But there. It's easy to poke fun at the planners. Put ourselves in their place, and what could we come up with half so good as the Portuguese permanent way, so much of which, doubtless under the stimulus of parties from Swindon, Derby and Crewe, is now under conversion from single gauge to broad, a source of fascination to those laymen on the trip who've wondered all their lives just how things work out at the point of changeover? No, I feel strongly that anyone with a helpful new idea should put it forward.

The travel people themselves are called in to say why our stretch covers wouldn't stretch—two sizes too small, that didn't take long—was just back from a week in a Greek villa where there was no furniture. Here's a wide field. Upholsterers of either sex, painfully backward in, say, Nepalese cushion-stuffing technology, could be breaking a leg to join your study and travel group on how to up-end heavy pieces without a rupture, and even if the Everest timetable permits—pretty packed at the moment—you could bet a few dozen winched up the south col for a whacking supplement, as an added attraction.

That's one of the advantages of these specialist operations. You can tack on any secondary activity you fancy, from Sohos of the World (or Topless in Gaza), to a grand, three-centre, car-cleaning contest, first man to beat the dents out of an Istanbul taxi gets a free swim of the Hellespont.

But you can't expect me to fiddle out all the details. You're the professionals. I'm just getting the ideas for you, as when I asked a guitar-player the other day, as he performed illegally in Green Park tube station, if he'd ever wanted to take up being an urban guerila. It put a hiccup in his Burt Bacharach, but his eyes lit up all right. Simulate a bit of street warfare somewhere for an Urban Guerilla Holiday, and you'd be laughing.

An what about the Topical Tour, an entirely unexplored field so far? Difficulties with the advance planning, naturally. Can't see the way things might be going next year. But this year, with the idea waiting to spring, you'd have been packing them off in their hundreds to look at the residence of Dr. Dan Ellsberg's psychiatrist, say, not to mention Capt. Mark Phillips. Just open the mind. Let the stuff float in.

Finally, leaving aside, for lack of space, such passing thoughts as Great Tunnels of the Western World, an idea put to me, if indirectly, last night, by a ticket inspector on the 12.28 from Victoria, as we both passed the time stuck deep down under the South Downs with the lights out, also a run round the Unsolved Crimes of the Bahamas or guaranteed eye-witnessing of a sun-drenched, bloodless coup in Bogota, some place like that, let's not forget that Do-it-Yourself, contrary to best-informed speculations, is still with us.

Coach them out to a Gobi waterhole and leave them there with a fortnight's packed lunches, is all you need.

Get the money first, though. Not that you ever don't.

The Complete
Crowd-Lover's Guide

A is for AGORAPHOBIA Agoraphobia is a small Mediterranean island near Majorca, where tourism has boomed so wonderfully that there is not one square inch of the island that does not have a hotel standing, or sometimes falling, on it. It is, in consequence, highly prized by the British, who have a hatred of lying in the sun, preferring to be wedged upright in it.

B is for BEACH For those unable to manage an Agoraphobian holiday this year, many British beaches can be almost as diverting, offering as they do unrivalled opportuntiies for having sand kicked in your face and small boys peeing on your sandal to the shriek of a thousand trannies left unattended while their teenage owners make nonsense of the age of consent mere inches from the deckchair you have just lost an eye fighting for.

C is for CINEMA For the genuine crowd-lover, there is little to compare with sitting in the dark being coughed on by the bronchitics that make up 98.7% of all cinema audiences. A high point of the evening always comes five minutes after the start of the film when the bronchitics get up and begin treading on your feet, knocking your glasses off with their overcoats, and dripping loganberry ripple on your trousers.

D is for DISCOTHEQUE Discotheque is a French medical term used to describe the sensation of being dropped into the engine room of the *Titanic* just at that moment when the cattle in the forward hold have realised the implications of *Abide With Me* and are running through it to get at the Chief Engineer.

E is for ERETHISM This office does not enter into personal correspondence, but a full list of rush hours is available from London Transport, on request.

F is for FAIRGROUNDS There is nothing like an honest English bank holiday fair with its slither of dead goldfish underfoot, its hands sheared off and seeping on the dodgem rink, its heady atmosphere of rancid frankfurter and flying floss-fleck, and the feathery caress of alien fingers on your wallet-pocket as, wedged among a throng of Hell's Angels, you are borne effortlessly onto machinery designed to make you throw up for money. It is what Easter is all about.

G is for GREGARIOUSNESS Gregariousness comes from the Latin *grex*, meaning flock, and it describes that warm, wonderful quality of many human beings which makes them indistinguishable from sheep.

H is for HYSTERIA Hysteria is one of the more engaging diversions which may be enjoyed in crowds, particularly when taken in conjunction with

I is for IDOL, which is something which periodically flies into London in order to enable crowds to engage in the foregoing. By some curious process known only to marketing science, an idol can not only fill a giant stadium with hysterical weeping teeny-boppers, it can also give them something to *really* weep about, such as crushed ribs, asphyxia, and disillusion.

J is for JUMBO JET For the really adventurous crowd-lover, nothing may match the delights of the jumbo jet, which is a box for taking four hundred people up to forty thousand feet and making them watch *The Sound of Music* for the eighth time while simultaneously wondering where civilization is going. The really fortunate gregophile, of course, will be doing this in a further crowd of twenty *other* jumbo jets, all circling Kennedy Airport.

K is for KOW-TOW The dictionary defines kow-tow as "the Chinese custom of touching the ground with the forehead as a sign of worship". It does not explain where nine hundred million people find the room to do it.

L is for LONDON According to Samuel Johnson, "when a man is tired of London, he is tired of life." That was the sort of crack you could get away with in 1770, when the city contained 600,000 people; as it now contains 10,000,000, you can see why Johnson carries less weight than he once did. His statue is in the Strand, by the way, and has eighteen people living on it.

M is for MOUNTAINS Fortunately for crowd-lovers, mountains are not now the dreary escapes to solitude they once were, and well worth the climb for those wishing to share a peak with Chris Bonnington, Don Whillans, Joe Brown, Dougal Haston, Mike Burke, two BBC Outside Broadcast teams, two hundred aspirants to a Duke of Edinburgh Award, and sixty-eight beautiful people filming a commercial for Dubonnet-flavoured toothpaste.

N is for NUDIST COLONY One for crowd-haters, this; no better therapy exists than a nice bare throng.

O is for OPERA Opera represents the highest expression of crowding as an art form. Opera is where one thousand people squeeze, immaculately dressed for the occasion, into a small bar to cover one another in champagne and jump up and down in the hope of identifying other members of the crowd. In the intervals, you can relax by sitting down and listening to music.

P is for PUBS Pubs are a sort of working-class opera. What you get covered in is beer; other people's on the way to the bar, your own on the way back. A tip: never clear a path with your glass; hold it against your chest with one hand, and shove a corridor with the other. It's what your right arm's for.

Q is for QUEENS Queens are the highest form of crowd-lover. What all queens dread most is going to the window one morning and seeing nothing but one Jap at the railings asking the sentry if this is Carnaby Street.

R is for RESTAURANTS Nothing compares with the pleasure of a truly crowded restaurant, especially one where the tables are so close together that your neighbour's pea flies into your wine while his companion, throwing herself back the better to laugh uproariously at his rotten old joke simultaneously shoves you into your soup. If you have any, that is; many popular restaurants close before you've managed to catch the waiter's eye.

S is for SHOPS And, of course, for SALES, which represent the the high point of the crowd-lover's year, when he has all the fun of fighting for something he doesn't want with someone he doesn't know for money he hasnt' got. The joy of coming home with half a pyjama leg and a black eye cannot be described.

T is for TRAFFIC Gottlieb Daimler (1834-1900), the great German crowd-lover, dedicated himself to the dream of inventing something which would enable mobs of people to congregate at great speed; and finally came up with the motor car. That they would one day be able to become a motionless pack on the very road itself, without the need to go anywhere else to do it, was, of course, beyond his wildest expectations.

U is for UTI POSSIDETIS The principle that leaves belligerents in possession of what they have acquired. It can be used of deck-chairs, parking spots, spaces at the bar, railway compartments, queues, anything or anywhere, in short, where two or more crowd-lovers have met and fought to a finish.

V is for VISITORS TO THESE SHORES The friendly way of describing tourists. Tourists are wandering mobs of vandals who invade Britain in their millions, grab the best seats, tables, taxis, goods, and women, and clog every square foot of countryside. Visitors To These Shores are importers of foreign currency.

W is for WINTERSPORTS See under MOUNTAINS, except that's exactly what you can't do, the lower slopes being filled with queues of frozen human beings in incalculably expensive gear waiting to be hooked onto a conveyor belt and taken to the upper slopes in order to collide with one another on the way down again, this being the best way of throwing parties in South Kensington where people come in and sign your legs.

X is for XENOPHOBIA The native name for AGORAPHOBIA.

Y is for YARD In America, a yard is a vast expanse attached to one's house, often with an Olympic pool in it. In Britain, it is something containing three feet, but only if the householder has remembered to remove his shoes and curl the toes to fit. The other foot belongs to his neighbour, much of whose own yard has been sold for exciting office development.

Z is for ZOOID The dictionary defines a zooid as something of an animal nature, either separate or a compound organism with manifest animal characteristics. It would therefore go on to define it as both a crowd and the individual people in it, if it weren't on the last page and space hadn't run out. As it will for everyone.

"I think he's saying that it's upside down."

There is Some Corner of a Foreign Pub

GRAHAM on the British landlord abroad

"Remember that glorious autumn evening when we strolled out from the hotel, and saw the A VENDRE notice?"

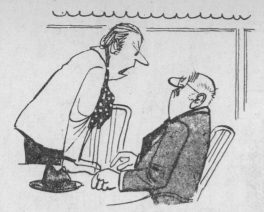

"*Don't garçon me, mate!*"

"*God, it's good to get out of the rat-race.*"

"*Par exemple, on commence avec vingt double—alors . . .*"

"Charterhouse—ecole Anglaise."

"Sometimes I wonder if we wouldn't have been better sinking our savings in that motor repair business in Leamington."

Sight for Sore Eyes

If it's Wednesday, this must be ALAN BRIEN who is seeing things

YOU can never win as a sight-seer. Somebody else, more often than not the first person you meet when you get back home, has been there before you. And it turns out you weren't in the right place anyway. The Taj Mahal by moonlight? Well, it's all right for trippers, coach tours, those who like to stick to the beaten track, but for his money, which is always more than your money, the real sight to see is the Agate Mosque of Ali Hassan the Effulgent, just round the corner though, of course, almost impossible to find unless you have the right contacts, where the lapis-lazuli dome has been known to levitate, though only on the second Wednesday in Ramadan when it coincides with the monsoon.

There is invariably another church in Venice, just a few bridges across a few canals further on, where the marble draperies are even finer; another temple more fantastic than Ankor-Wat though unfortunately under terrorist mortar bombardment on your visit; another section on your visit; another section of the Hermitage in Leningrad open only to those who carry a letter from the British Ambassador, another waterfall, a hundred miles deeper into the hinterland, which you could have reached if you had possessed the foresight to carry with you a 10 lb. bag of salt for the headman, and not been too squeamish to mix your blood in brotherhood with the head-hunters. You should always have been there last year—before it was ruined by tourists like you.

Just to admit that you went out there to see the sights is to tie a label round your neck reading "Tourist Class". It is clear that you stay in hotels where you actually meet people who speak English, that you use taxis when you are not commuting in the airport bus, that you have to look up things in guide books. You are the sort of character who only gets to foreign parts on your annual vacation. The First Person is never a holiday-maker. He is a traveller. He has "spent a few weeks" everywhere, when he hasn't actually "lived there for a year or two just after the war".

While you may have been taken round the stately home, he has stayed there as "a house-guest". (Are there "garden-guests"? "Potting-shed guests"? "Garage-guests"?) He has slept in the Sir Walter Raleigh bed, eaten off the silver-plated gold dinner service, taken his night-cap every night in the presence of the Rubens *Bacchus and His Rout*. He is always among friends, wherever he is, who send the chauffeur to meet his plane and give him the use of the car during his stay. He doesn't have to look at the scenery, he is part of it, having bought up a dozen acres of beauty spot when it was going cheap at £120 the plot. He doesn't read the guide book—if he didn't write it, then he's mentioned in it.

He's always arriving somewhere, but you rarely see him leave. Or if you do, he's not on his way home, loaded with souvenirs, coral fronds, turtle shells, temple bells, carvings of elephants, but on his way to somewhere else. He's the man who brings things in to other places, Gentleman's Relish, Cooper's Oxford marmalade, a brace of Purdies, shoes from Lobbs, shirts from Turnbull & Asser, for the residents.

You can't compete with the First Person—you, who never go anywhere twice, who have only one jaunt abroad for every year of your working life; who only read the brochures, as motorists read car ads, after you have spent your money in order to reassure yourself it was worth the outlay. The best protective ploy is to collect sights that no one else collects.

It may not be the most rewarding monologue you have ever rehearsed in the bath, but if you can compare and contrast, say, sewage systems in two hemispheres, preferably with slides, then at least you know you have got there ahead of everybody else. There are more congenial anthologies you can compile. Vincent Mulchrone collects bars—or do they collect him?—around the world. No man better equipped to settle an argument on where to find the coolest beer or the warmest barmaid, the best-placed foot-rail or the softest sofa, or what goes into and comes out of a Purple Hurricane. Alan Coren makes straight for the local estate agent and has been inside more private mansions under false pretences in strange climes than even the local burglar, or the local secret police.

I collect markets—if you can't find a place where nobody goes, then at least here everybody comes. My first was in Bordeaux, that vast, glass-roofed casserole where fruit and sea food tower up on all sides, as shiny, new and playful as a toy shop at Christmas. My last was in Georgetown, Guyana, like a Wild West railway station during a gold bonanza, corridors of packing cases, dark and narrow as Soho alleyways, where vendors sit all day in plywood kraals, offering three tomatoes, an onion and an eggplant on a single wilting cabbage leaf.

People are what they eat—all the more what they buy and sell. Even in the Soviet Union, no one can fake a market to hoodwink the visitor, and I saw there, in Tashkent and in Riga, anywhere except Moscow, some of my favourite sights—from Arab-style souks, with kebabs on real swords, men taking offers for the turbans off their heads, beans like Rajah's jewels, to ultra-hygenic refrigerated, air-conditioned emporia, like operating theatres, where I would cheerfully have laid down on a spotless slab to have my tonsils out.

There is a little secret pocket of capitalism in the most socialist heart. And in markets, you find the magic of supply and demand, proving that somebody will inevitably buy anything in the end if the price is right. Wherever they are they have an atmosphere in common which survives despite temperature, politics, race or religion.

It is like a warm-up for a carnival—the corrupt, luxurious, intoxicating smell of over-ripe fruit squashing underfoot to an impromptu punch; the itch in your nose from charring meat, peppery spices, ancient, under-the-floorboard herbs, aromatic juices which make your eyes run; the assault on the ears of the hubble-bubbling, twanging, fluting voices like an orchestra perpetually tuning up; the rhythmic, pulsating pressure of people on all sides, who'd rather look at a forked radish, a snake hamburger or pair of sandals made out of genuine Goodyear tyre, than at you, so that you feel you are part of some mass, shuffling dance; and the fever-dream dazzle of visual impressions, faces like turnip masks, turnips like severed heads, strings and pyramids and loops and armies and pillars of objects that you could never imagine somebody could possibly imagine somebody else needing.

That's what I call sight-seeing. Ten minutes is about all I can manage for the most spectacular mountain or bay. A couple of hours for your castle, or church, or palace, or hydro-electric dam. But in the market I could sit for days, fantasying myself Sandy Arbuthnot or other Imperial Buchanesque secret agent disguised as a fakir or a water-carrier.

"Good grief, it's the wife!"

No Robins on the Palm Trees

ALAN WHICKER'S flying Christmas

I'M a Silent Night man myself, prepared to settle for things just the way the cards are dealt: robins and snow and stage-coaches and hot punch outside firelit Tudor mansions and rosy-cheeked retainers touching forelocks and all those things everybody *else* always has at this time of year.

So why do I spend Christmas as the only passenger in a 350-seat Jumbo with a morose cabin crew of eighteen watching me masticate plastic pudding? Why do I land at Cayenne when the airport is closed on Christmas Eve and taxis don't return until Thursday week? Why do Congolese Immigration ask me to Step This Way when they should be offering toddy toasts and sending me glowing into the palmy night—don't they *know* about Goodwill to All Men, with or without visas?

The whole Holly Scene has a habit of passing me by while I'm struggling to convince Thai revolutionaries that to get home in time I should be on that jet at the end of the runway, the one with the flashing lights. After all, why should Christmas be something I only read about?

I once spent the whole festive season in the Canal Zone, which never was Instant Dingley Dell. The Israelis were fighting only us, then, while the Egyptians put a match to Shepherds Hotel, dismissed Farouk to his Roman dolce vita, threw a few Britons out of Turf Club windows and disembowelled them in the streets. Goodwill was thin on the ground.

The British Army was protecting (would you believe?) the Suez Canal. We were not yet accredited War Correspondents so the military refused to entertain us within their guarded Moascar base outside Ismailia, but shrugged us off into the distant United Services Club. We weren't expecting jolly old Santa to come down that unprotected chimney; what infidels were liable to get for Christmas, yo ho ho, was a fellaheen's rusty knife between the ribs.

The Army, knowing out-of-sight meant out-of-responsibility, despatched us to the Club by armoured car before scuttling back to Base, leaving a bewildered collection of unarmed British, French and American Correspondents bolting themselves in to spend Christmas with the unexpired portion of the year's beer, fresh from the Star Brewery, Cairo, and tins of NAAFI sausages piled high.

The Club stood the wrong side of the Sweetwater Canal—and you can't get any wronger than that. The turgid moat which Ismailians used for washroom, lavatory and drinking brimmed with dead dogs and refuse. "Death from the bougainvillaea!" we used to write when passing people got shot-up along Suicide Mile; yes, we had a neat turn of headline.

On Christmas Eve we settled down to make merry in a bare bar softened only by unlimited beer and a dartboard. It wasn't Dickensian but it *was* safe. Well, you have to believe what they tell you.

I hadn't even got my double before a shattering fusillade hit the outside wall and, worse yet, priceless bottles of good cheer lay smashed. When the shouting died down and the AFP man had spread cups around to collect dripping cognac it transpired that, from the minaret above a nearby mosque, our unfriendly neighbourhood sniper had the well-lit dartboard firmly in his telescopic sights. It was only by the grace of Allah and an instinctive lack of markmanship that he failed to double-top us. This is *Christmas?*

Darts went by the board. We wished him the Season's Greeting and, muttering, settled for poker in an inside room without windows, letting nothing us dismay. The game continued until Boxing Day; it's one way to pass the hols when the fellaheen are unfriendly.

Play had added zest for me because of an AP man called Tom Stone who began his professional career as a dealer in a Reno casino. To learn that curious craft he spent ten hours a day dealing cards to himself in front of a mirror; as a result he could do anything with a

"This is the last time we come to Spain. You've spent the entire holiday worrying how they can afford to do it at the price."

deck before your very eyes—the walking, talking Awful Warning about playing cards with strangers.

He would announce he was going to cheat, shuffle, let the deck be cut, and deal. While everybody watched, transfixed, he'd give himself four aces and more important, make sure somebody else had a full-house (no point in fixing a good hand if nobody bets . . .). Because of this fatal fluency he would not touch the cards in a friendly game, but passed the deal. As he'd known the percentages since he was so high, he always won. I learnt a lot, sitting on his left hand; best to see how *he* was going to bet before pushing-in my paltry piastres . . .

There was another interesting Christmas in the red dead heart of Australia, between Alice Springs and Darwin. The Alice may be small but Tennant's Creek smaller. At the main pub I was offered a comfy bed with five other Single Gents. I can be convivial, but I know about Outback nights and the Technicolor yawn, so tried again a couple of miles up the highway. There was Room at the Inn all right—seventeen, sharing. What with that and Christmas pudding at 110 in the shade, the Pickwickian pictures stayed out of focus .. .

For a really white Christmas there's always Alaska and Nome, on the Bering Straits just across from Russia. As I always say, there's no place like Nome. The hotel was a quick-lunch counter, with beds, and full of celebrating Eskimos. At Christmas they should be tradi-tionally easy to take, like polar bears, but these were bananas about Elvis Presley. He had just reached the Arctic Circle, and they kept him belting out of the juke-box all night. I tried to settle-down upstairs but the thump of the double-bass vibrated the bed-springs; I couldn't hear the melody but I got the throb, just behind the eyes. Never felt quite the same again about Nanook.

That Christmas I flew North to Point Barrow with Director Jack Gold. We had come over the Pole from Copenhagen and bounced up from Anchorage in a U.S. Army DC3. Point Barrow is the end of the world, and I do mean. The sea freezes for ten long, dark months and you can walk to the North Pole, if you want to go that way.

We stepped from the rickety Dak and discovered my suitcase had been left in the Anchorage hotel lobby. When Arctic winds from Santa's storeroom whistle through the Y's, I'm here to say no gents 13oz. natty can handle the festive season North of the Dew Line. You can't make merry when you're wondering about your frozen limit.

I've been hit by that accompanied-baggage double-shuffle before. I used to pack jackets in the large case, trousers in the small until, arriving in Lagos, the airline announced the small case had gone on to the next country. My immaculate jackets were present, but no immaculate trousers; not easy to be traditionally British when you've lost your better half and feel like Carry On up the Niger.

That's all in the past but as I keep saying, I know exactly the way Christmas ought to be, truly I do, so why are there no robins in this palm tree? What happened to the holly? Why do those Tontons Macoutes keep staring? Are you *sure* that's a cracker? What's the Haitian for Happy Christmas, sir . . .?

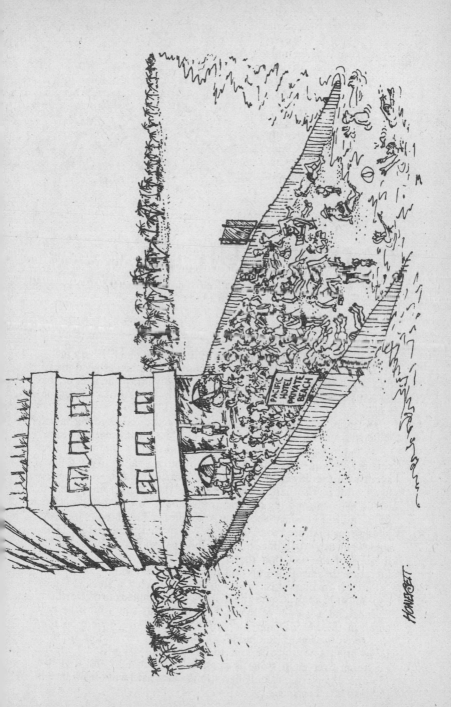

FIRST,
CATCH YOUR MAN. . .

A few recipes for holiday romance from ANN LESLIE

GOD did not design me for the European summer. If you really want to know and I don't suppose you do, he designed me to be a sex-symbol in Tonga, where they rightly scorn the idea of the pocket Venus, preferring something more on the scale of a Gladstone bag.

The loins of Tonga manhood refuse to stir for anything much under thirteen stone or a 40C cup: they like their women to come in the handy jumbo-sized pack. Thus it was that I found myself one summer sprinting coyly from palm grove to copra factory and back again with the flower of Tongan youth in hot pursuit—a dedicated band of dusky Lotharios who, whenever they panted into earshot, would begin murmuring one to another about how my belly was like unto an heap of wheat set about with lilies and my breasts like two young roes that are twins, and other such pretty fol-de-rols. (This somewhat derivative line in erotic chit-chat was entirely forgivable in view of the fact that the Song of Solomon was the feelthiest literature then available on that mission-ridden isle.)

Summer in Europe is, for the likes of me, alas, a somewhat less ego-boosting affair. Come June, and a plug is pulled out of Northern Europe and a stream of lissom blondes floods south into the oily sump of the Med. Stripped down, lubricated with Ambre Solaire, and given the final fashionable tan finish, they're ready in no time to be fitted as optional extras to the season's drop-head Ferraris. Anything over eight stone is apparently rejected by the Riviera's motorised playboys, if only because the increased wind-resistance is liable to affect torque.

(Incidentally it may come as a surprise—at least to the mini-Mastroiannis who flare their tiny nostrils at the Nordic goddesses strewn amidst the sewage and coke bottles of the typical Riviera beach—that there actually do exist Swedish girls who are short, fat, dark and spotty. Mercifully for Mediterranean manhood, some invisible filter stretched across the Skaggerak sieves them out and only the blondes fall through to the south. The short dark fatties presumably spend their summers mooching suicidally about in Scandinavian pinewoods, sheltering from that vicious wind which whips in off the Baltic like a high-speed bacon-slicer . . .)

The first time I set my girlish footprint on sinful Continental soil was on a school safari round the Loire chateaux under the doughty duenna-ship of one Mother Consolata. Mother C. and a bullet-like glare which could fell a man at fifty paces, wielded a mean rosary, and was destined for a dazzling career as a nightclub bouncer—had the Lord not, somewhat inexplicably, chosen her to be His Bride instead.

Oh my paws and whiskers, I muttered as I gasped about in her wake like the White Rabbit, oh for the day when I could cast her and my liberty-bodice aside for good, and hie me in search of sin in St. Tropez. O.K., so a passion for spam fritters and iced buns has given me the physique of your average Latvian street-cleaner. But what matter, since *I* was not going to try to compete on the vulgar level of mere buttock and boob. No, indeed. Finer-qualities-beneath-the-fleshly-dross was to be my winning ploy.

With a sad, but amused, curl of my Mona Lisa lip, and by the elegant way I toyed with the pages of Proust and let fall the odd Pensée from Pascal, I would subtly convey the impression of a woman with a Full Rich Inner Life—rather than of one who on the whole, could barely restrain the impulse to sink her jealous fangs into the passing ankles of bikinied rivals.

One day, I felt sure, I would find myself conversing soulfully on the poop-deck of some glistening yacht with the world-weary scion of a Bolivian tin dynasty (whom Life had made bitter, but who was Basically Worthwhile). And, suddenly, the scales would fall from his eyes and he'd realise that there beside him, under the calamine lotion and horsefly repellent, he had discovered the Good Woman to be prized above rubies.

After a mad, passion-filled night spent grappling with each other betwixt rose-scented sheets, we'd greet the southern dawn with sated smiles of love, and he'd be as lithe and brown as a water god and I would be—well, as presentable as could be expected in the circs, having remembered to weld on my Mary Quant "Make Up to Make Love In" the night before so as not to look like the small crushed pig I normally resemble in the morning. Yes, that's how it would be . . . .

Yes, that's how it bloody well wasn't. When I finally got there years later, I discovered that a Good Woman with a Full Rich Inner Life is a guaranteed non-starter in the St. Tropez Stakes, unless she also happens to have a waist like a stick-insect and a pair of legs which start up around her arm-pits. If my tin-rich water dog was anywhere, he was in that jostling stampede of seedy off-duty waiters

143

and Brylcreemed Italian bank-clerks fighting for the favours of topless temps on the Tahiti-Plage. Short of shackling his ankles or concussing him with my Proust, I clearly hadn't a hope of catching him.

In the event I had to settle for a portly young works manager from Stuttgart who was homeseick for the generous curves of Westphalian womanhood and who evidently proposed to seduce me over a gargantuan meal and flagons of lust-inducing wine served on a trolley in his room.

Alas for poor Helmut, the feast was his undoing, if not mine: while polishing off his final brandy and revving up to the rape at last he suddenly fell face-down on the grand-lit as if shot by a sniper and promptly sank into a pale, death-like sleep. Next day, I shook the sand of St. Trop from my toes, never to return again.

Of course Europe does provide resorts where you don't have to spend your time competing for the booby-prize in some relentless sexual rat-race. For example, you can always take your tender ego off to the Costa Geriatrica of Lake Lucerne, and there have it soothed by the sounds of lapping water, colliding crutches and the occasional slow-motion pile-up of wheel-chairs on the prom.

Or you can deposit yourself in the sub-tropical heat of a conservatory in some broken-down Apennine spa, where yellowing parcels of papery flesh, held together by mufflers and propped up in raffia chairs, await the Last Trump amidst the sweating ferns. Here, any woman, so long as she's got a set of limbs in more or less working order and doesn't have to unhinge her teeth and park them overnight in a glass, qualifies as an instant Lolita. (And as such she's liable to get chucked out by the management for being a "disruptive element", whose stimulating effect on ancient libidos might well produce a terminal experience among the frailer specimens of the clinetèle.)

But these are counsels of despair. If man-hunting is really your bag, it's best to head for places like Mexico City or Rome where the male inhabitants are absurdly indiscriminate and react like moggies to catnip at the sight of anything female between the ages of eight and eighty. Since so many Italian women look like scrumptious little honey-pots, you may wonder why their menfolk can be bothered to go buzzing about after any other variety. The answer lies in the tendency for the Italian female to jump the gun and start introducing young Carlo to everyone as her "fidanzato" after only the second date. And since Italian girls tend to own posses of glowering, hot-blooded brothers, who are liable to take it amiss if the putative "fidanzato" insults family honour by trying to wriggle off the hook, the Italian male feels much safer pressing his charms on girls with return tickets to Oslo.

You may of course fancy that you're intelligent and mature enough to sit out the absurd sexual square dance of the European summer hols, and if so, bully for you. But once the music strikes up and the command goes out to "Take your partners please," are you sure you'll still be saying "No, no, I'm only here for the Berninis"?

Fifteen Days in Sunsoaked Errata

Never heard of the place? SHERIDAN MORLEY raves about it

FOR those of us who believed that travel brochures were the last great resting place of romantic fiction, it is proving a difficult summer.

In the past, the procedure for real holiday sadists had a classical simplicity and purity about it; towards the end of May, you armed yourself from any large travel agency with a stack of four-colour booklets relating to foreign parts with which you actually happened to be familiar. That achieved, most of June and July could then be spent prostrate in a Berkshire garden, chortling happily over the Pimms and the differences between what the brochures described and what you knew hundreds of misguided tourists were at that moment enduring.

Alas, no more: since the arrival of the Trades Descriptions Act and the almost simultaneous realisation that Spanish hotels didn't have to be collapsible, a terrible truthfullness has descended on the writers and, what's worse, on the photographers involved with travel brochures. No longer is it possible to find the same well-travelled girl clutching the same daiquiri on the sands of St Tropez and then mysteriously reappearing a few pages later with precisely the same glass on the sands of Lloret de Mar; no longer is it even possible to visualise that benighted hack in a garret above Victoria Street ransacking his imagination for glowing descriptions of a hotel he's never seen for the simple reason that it's still having its foundations laid at the time of his deadline.

In the cause of accuracy, not to mention immunity from prosecution, the colour has gone out of the brochure business and we are left with the unedifying spectacle of tour operators desperately containing their fantasies within the realms of possibility—or, still worse, following up their brochures with pages of amendments and errata admissions, bringing us back to earth with a sickening thud.

But is it really necessary? Was it essential, for example, for Greek Island Holidays to admit, under the heading "additional information", that contrary to what was suggested by their 1973 booklet, at the Hotel Metropolitan Capsis in Rhodes:

"There is no Swedish style solarium. There is no children's playground. Although there is a Conference Room, which is also used as a Cinema, and there is projection equipment, we understand that the Hotel Management have not bought any films nor made provision to hire films. There is no gymnasium although limited exercise facilities are available in the Sauna Room. There is no Library. The area referred to as such by the hotel would more correctly be described as a Correspondence Room which forms part of the Lounge. There is no Beauty Salon. There is no roof garden nightclub. There is a Bar/Lounge on the

roof where music, piped or piano, is played but there is no area for dancing. Most rooms have sea-view."

Wouldn't it really have been more fun to get there and then find all that out? After all it might have taken days to discover everything that was missing, even assuming you had kept the brochure for reference, and by that time the Management might have located a film library in the neighbourhood or flown in Philip Jenkinson from Television Centre.

Forewarnings of this kind severely limit the potential for rows with the Manager and are inclined to jeopardise those stormy baggage-clutching departures which are the stuff all true holiday-makers' dreams are made of. It's not even as though things are any better at the Grand Hotel in Rhodes ("*We have been advised that the hotel has utilised the area where the tennis courts used to be for further developments. However, for those wishing to play tennis the hotel will make arrangements for them with the Rhodes Tennis Club. Although the beach is directly in front of the hotel, it is not private. The swimming pool is smaller than Olympic size*") and as for the nearby Hotel Chevaliers Palace:

"*There is no Swedish style solarium but there is a small terrace by the swimming pool and a roof garden which is often used for sun-bathing. As yet there is no boutique.*"

After all, what's a boutique between friends? Still, if you feel strongly then you'd better be a bit careful about Greek Islands' offerings in Corfu too: take the Nissaki Beach Hotel:

"*The gymnasium, sauna bath and squash court proposed for 1973 have not yet been installed. We cannot guarantee that they will be available this summer.*"

The Corcyra Beach Hotel isn't perfect either ("*It should be noted that the buffet lunches are only served in the restaurant by the swimming pool from May to September*") but then what fool would want to eat his Christmas lunch by a Greek swimming pool anyway? As for what constitutes an Olympic-size pool, opinions seem to vary between London and Glyfada. At the Grand Hotel:

"*There is no tennis court. The swimming pool is in fact smaller than Olympic size.*

Still, who's measuring? And anyway, at least it's better than Crete (anything is better than Crete) where at the Hotel Coral: "*There is no swimming pool.*" How about the Ariadni Beach Hotel? "*The beach in front of this hotel is mainly pebble, but with sand below the water line.*"

Right then, enough of messing about on the islands, how about Athens, the Hotel Semiramis?

"*Please note that the beaches of Glyfada and Nea Makri, although not 'magnificent', are pleasant but are respectively some 17 and 30 kilometres away.*"

But then one man's magnificence is another's pleasure and we all have our problems, particularly Greek hoteliers in midseason; why not try a villa—the Alexia, for instance, in Corfu:

"*Whilst this villa is in a peaceful position, it is situated close to another villa and is not isolated.*"

So it's seclusion you want? The Villa Persephone then:

"*This villa is approximately twenty minutes walk from the village.*"
Better yet, those trying to get right away from it all, including most of the rest of their families, could try the Villas Thetys and Neptune:

"*It should be noted that these villas are approached by steps and are therefore not suitable for the infirm or the very young.*"

On a diet? What about Ay Gordis then:

"*As advised in the Corfu A-Z section of the brochure, there is no electricity in Ay Gordis. The cooker and refrigerator work off calor gas or oil, lighting is by oil lamps. We regret the Taverna owner will no longer offer the facility of taking meals to the villas.*"

But even here there seems to be an air of prosaic literalism creeping in: take the Villa Amoudra in Crete for instance:

"*This villa overlooks the sea, not the beach which is approximately ten minutes walk away.*"

On second thoughts, maybe you'd better not take it: as for the Villas Stella, Effi and Flora (a superb music-hall trio now apparently in the travel business) on Rhodes:

"*A sea view can only be obtained from the roofs of these villas.*"

Meanwhile, back at the Villa Flora:

"*The sitting area does not lead to the bathroom and kitchen. These are on the far side of a small private courtyard.*"

Positive thinking, that's what's needed; on the Paxos page for instance, instead of announcing of one Taverna that:

"*Accommodation at this taverna has been withdrawn as renovation work has not progressed; however we have been able to obtain some rooms over the local Post Office.*"

How much better it would have been to inform the clients that in order to facilitate postcard-sending the Paxos accommodation had moved to a more central location, to which could have been added the alluring information that on a clear day on the Paxos post-office steps it is often possible to see Peter Bull sending off his entry for the *Sunday Mirror's* Spot-the-Ball competition.

Anyway, have a happy holiday; me, I'm off back to the garden with the rest of the brochures.

"*. . . and over here, we have the ruined Abbot of Lindisfarne.*"

"Seeing we are here, I thought we might as well open a new branch."

Have Subsidiary, Must Travel

MAHOOD looks at those executives whose firms have little companies conveniently situated in winter holiday resorts

"I knew it was too good to last—now the shop stewards want to pay an annual visit to our little firm in Miami."

"*Mr. Hendon, you've forgotten your reason for going!*"

"'*Marvellous weather, wish you were here, Regards. Sam.'*
When we get back to the U.K., Miss Marbon, remind me
that this branch needs a Xerox."

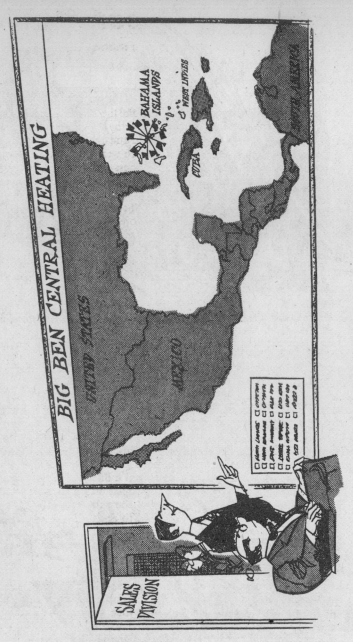

"It's a tough area to crack so we concentrate all our best men at that branch once a year."

Travelling Hopefully

LORD MANCROFT *reports from a waiting room
somewhere abroad*

THIS was their Captain speaking from the flight deck, and his voice was meaningful and leaderworthy. "Folks," he said, "I have two pieces of noos for you, one good and one bad. First the bad, We're lost. And now for the good, We're well ahead of Skedool." The air hostess reassumed her air hostess smile, and everybody relaxed. They had been taken into Captain Bobbliwobski's confidence, and all was therefore well.

This, I feel, is the correct approach when things are going agley, and they are bound to go agley even more as travel becomes daily more precipitate and international travel regulations more enigmatic. Breakfast in London, luncheon in New York, and luggage in Los Angeles—I'm surprised that chaos doesn't occur more frequently than it does. But people will not mind being diverted from Glasgow to the Gobi Desert if only you tell them what's happening. Tell them the delay is due to "operational reasons" and they'll all suspect that the Captain is drunk.

My views on this point were shared by the Station-master at Spagthorpe Junction. On a memorable occasion I remember him announcing that the train then standing at Platform 1 was the train, whereas the train then arriving at Platform 2 was the Flying Scotsman which had frankly taken them all slightly by surprise.

It was also the attitude of the man in the queue at the time of the recent hi-jacking scare. It was of course a nuisance having to turn up at the airport two hours before take-off in order to be ransacked by an embarrassed teenage policeman, but we all saw the point. Nobody likes to find himself in mid-Atlantic sitting next to a fellow traveller whose underwear is full of hand grenades.

The Customs gentlemen, of course, boil a different kettle of fish. Getting through the Customs has developed into a battle of wits, but with all this ecology going around the rules of the game are becoming complex. "Have you anything to declare, Sir? Any uncut diamonds, gold bullion, narcotics, obscene literature, beeswax, nasturtium seeds, bird feathers, or dried meat?" If you're only carrying the permitted quota of dried meat you're allowed out through the green door of the Customs Shed, but those who fear they may be overstocked with beeswax must go out through the red. This sensible procedure has speeded things up a lot, but woe betide you if you don't declare anything and then get caught in a spot check.

Aficionados will remember the case of the medical student from Villars-sur-Bex. The Customs gentleman at Gatwick bade him undo his Burberry presumably so that they could admire his waistcoat. This garment was subsequently found to contain 627 wrist watches, the existence of which V.-sur-B. had omitted to mention. The Customs gentlemen naturally disapproved of this oversight, and

"Are you sure we've been there? I shouldn't like to have missed it!"

so did the Recorder of London who granted V.-sur-B. four years in which to reconsider his attitude. In the course of cross-examination, Sir Godfrey Russell Vick, Q.C. (defending), asked one of the Customs officers how his suspicions had been aroused. Had there been a tip-off from the Swiss authorities? Had some fence squealed? Or was it just the professional expertise and natural acumen of the Gatwick Customs? The officer scratched for a moment with the toe oᶠ perplexity on the heel of embarrassment. "Sir Godfrey," he replied shyly, "it was none of these things. It had been a bumpy passage. They were self-winding watches, and the lad just stood there ticking like a plague of locusts."

By and large British Customs officials carry out a difficult task with courtesy and skill. So, indeed, do the Immigration authorities, though they have a more difficult task because politics enter into their game, and the stakes may be a good deal higher than with the Customs, particularly if you are trying to convince the officials that you are only one of a party of 137 East African Pakistani tourists seeking a week or two's respite in sun-drenched Wolverhampton.

In America the rules are even tougher. In spite of all that friendly welcome to "the huddled masses yearning to breathe free" which is inscribed round the Statue of Liberty, Uncle Sam has grown a bit touchy about so many of the Mafia coming to visit their relations, and the immigration form you have to fill up is pretty stringent. Just after the war it used to be even more searching. Gilbert Harding took exception to Question 7—"Do you intend to take up arms or offer violence against the Constitution of the U.S.A.?" "Sole purpose of visit" he declared firmly. But the Question I mylsef liked best was the last one of all that said, "In case you are illiterate you may ask for assistance in filling up this form."

As a matter of fact I never think the Americans need worry all that much about illegal immigrants. The normal process of arriving at J. F. Kennedy Airport ought to do as much to discourage them as any rules or red tape. What with stacking for two hours over the airport because the controllers are going slow, and trailing for three hours through the permanently temporary immigration hall because the clerks are going even slower, and then a journey on the airline courtesy coach which you hoped was going to take you from Panam via Branniff to United, but owing to your inability to undertsand the Bronx patois fetches you up outside the Ladies Lingerie Department of Saks Fifth Avenue, I think it's a miracle that anybody ever gets into the U.S.A. at all.

Mark you, we ourselves aren't always that brilliant when the interests of travellers and workers are in conflict. The tourists off Cunard's "Carinthia" were once held up for three hours at the Liverpool Landing Stage because mice had been found in the dockers' canteen and the staff were out on strike, presumably for danger money. No wonder the Mersey Docks and Harbour Board are in trouble.

The French, of course, tackle the problem of red tape with a Gallic logic. One of the hazards of the travel trade, in which I earn my living, is the extent of the old boy net. This can occasionally enmesh you. "Why, goodness me," exclaims the Timbuctoo Airlines man at Bermuda Airport, "didn't we meet at last year's ASTA Conference in Tokyo?" "Yes, indeed." "Then come and have a drink. Abdul here will look after your tickets and passport." It isn't until you are half-way to Rio that you realise your passport is still in Abdul's pocket.

The last time I performed this trick was at Le Bourget. When I realised what had happened I asked for the wayward passports to be registered on to me at the Poste Restante at Antibes. I duly went to collect them, only to be told by the Postmaster that by virtue of Sec. 52 of the 1927 Postal Code for the District of Alpes Maritimes a registered packet could not be handed over to a foreigner without production of his passport. Well, we could see which way this conversation was going, so my wife said, "Why not open the package yourself ? You'll find the passports inside." "I am forbidden," replied the Postmaster gravely, "to open a registered package without the permission of the consignee." "But I *am* the consignee," I patiently explained. "Possibly," said the Postmaster sticking to his guns, "but you can't prove it without producing your passport." "Well, then," said my wife, "couldn't it be accidentally opened?" At that moment Mme. la Poste emerged from the back of the office. "Yes, indeed," she replied with an admiring glance at my wife. "Under Sec. 27 of the Code any registered package that becomes accidentally opened in transit must be resealed in the presence of the consignee. This accident will now occur." She thumped the package smartly on the counter; it burst open, and out came the passports. Back into the envelope they went, and the package was duly handed over to my wife, for whom I bought a well-earned bottle of Krug '28 at La Bonne Auberge outside.

Motto. Take your wife with you if you have to travel a lot, and and are not good with regulations. And, incidentally, if she happens to be travelling anywhere without you and you want her back in a hurry, send her a copy of your local newspaper with a little paragraph cut out.

Boarding Now at the Gateway to Experience

GEORGE MIKES broadens his horizon

TRAVELLING is about as popular in today's world as the quadrille is in modern discothèques. In other words, not very. We have been misled by the fact that nowadays more people go from one place to another than ever before. But simply going from London to Paris, from Rome to Bangkok, from Tokyo to Frankfurt, only *resembles* travelling; not more and not less than a railway timetable or the telephone directory resembles a book. Post-war affluence started a migration compared with which the Great Migration of Peoples, or the subsequent journeying of Genghis Khan and his crew, look like the activities of a minor, provincial hiking club. A considerable section of humanity is constantly on the move: men of business rush around the world on the slightest provocation; the duty-free shops at Hong Kong, Suva or Honolulu airports are as well known to senior executives today as the tea-room of Crewe junction used to be to commercial travellers in a bygone age. Millions of people spend interminable winter evenings planning their summer holidays and, in July and August, off they go: hundreds of thousands of people are crowded together on lonely, quiet beaches known only and exclusively to the readers of the *Sunday Times* and the *Daily Telegraph:* millions queue up for lovely cups of English tea in undiscovered Spanish resorts—undiscovered except by the readers of the *Daily Mirror* and the *Sun.* There is little chance of getting away from it: the beaten track is almost as congested as off the beaten track. In all this movement, migration, toing and froing, people failed to notice that travelling, in the proper and formerly accepted sense of the word, had died a quiet death.

Travelling has, to all intents and purposes, been replaced by tourism. Tourism has several advantages over travelling and contains one riddle, too. I am going to solve that riddle for our readers. But first the advantages:

(1) Tourism is a major force in maintaining world peace. Nobody really cared for the old-fashioned, individual traveller in search of beauty, ancient cathedrals, world-famous pictures, Roman ruins and, first of all, people who were different from him. But all governments, however dictatorial, care for package tours. The Iron Curtain countries want capitalist tourists; Latin America has an insatiable thirst for the despised dollar. No war has ever been avoided because it was likely to kill people; many a war has been avoided because it was likely to kill the tourist trade. The Greek colonels seem to be brave like lions, afraid of nothing, except of a decrease in tourism. As far as Russia is concerned, all foreigners are spies: but spies (from hard-currency countries) are welcome today. Franco reprieved the six Basques a few weeks ago and I read innumerable explanations why he had done it. All conceivable reasons were put forward

except the real one: he knew that cruel obstinacy would have kept a few hundred thousand Britons and other Westerners away from Spain—and that would not do. Today the non-invasion of foreign tourists is more dreaded than the invasion of foreign armies used to be. The peace of the Middle East is in the balance because some Arab lands have already lost so many tourists that war would make no difference whatsoever.

(2) Tourism (unlike individual travelling) can solve all the economic problems of the world. According to an old and unkind saying the inhabitants of certain Eastern lands lived on pinching one another's washing. Scientists explained that this was economically impossible. But scientists, once again, were wrong. This method, as tourism shows, is quite feasible. Post-war affluence is on the wane but the package tour goes on flourishing. It seems that as long as poor, practically penniless, people keep visiting one another's countries they can keep one another rich. This is actually the Mikes Law of Economics: *overall poverty, if properly husbanded, can produce overall riches*.

(3) The last great disadvantage of old-fashioned travelling *vis-à-vis* tourism is that travelling broadens the mind. Who wants his mind broadened? Minds are worn narrow nowadays, that is the fashion. Ours is the age of the expert. The Renaissance man used to know a little of many things; the expert knows an awful lot of one thing or rather of one small segment of one thing. To be a good expert, which in most cases means to be of any good in your job, you need your mind narrowed. The ultimate glory of the packaged tour is that it narrows the mind.

The riddle I was referring to is this: why do people become tourists at all? I have mentioned some advantages but these are incidental, not sought for; few people care to promote world peace and fewer still world prosperity. Few would spend money on their brains, whether broadening or narrowing them.

There are, of course, many theories. Some go because others go. Once you are bitten by the bug you cannot resist. Tourism is three times as infectious as the 'flu. Others are in search of sunshine and they freely admit that they do not care for the natives of Spain, Greece, Jamaica or Asia Minor; neither do they want to learn what they call the lingo. (When they do learn it, it becomes Greek or Spanish or Turkish; when they are unwilling, or unable, to learn it, it remains the *lingo*.) Some go to check up on the guide-books: they want to see if the Mona Lisa is still smiling and if the Leaning Tower of Pisa is still leaning. Others go because they want to be photographed in front of the Akropolis, in St. Mark's Square or in front of the Taj Mahal. Others again just go to buy the necessary souvenirs. These, like the snapshot collectors, want *evidence* of their adventures. To be there is nothing; to have been there is the real glory.

The English, and this is my great discovery, go all over the world because they are nice, home-loving people. They go because they want to be at home; they go because they want to have decent English cups of tea in Tossa; crumpets in Sitges; bacon-and-egg-breakfasts in Palma and half a bitter in Corfu. They go because they love their neighbours and while they would not even look at them at home in Stockton-on-Tees they embrace them and have good heart-to-heart chats with them (about other people in their street) in Dubrovnik. They get up early every day in Estoril otherwise they might miss their *Daily Express*. They go abroad because they love England and their own people. At home they run into more and more foreigners, Americans, and coloured people; on the Costa Brava wherever they may look, they see true Britons only.

Those who regard themselves a shade more sophisticated, complain that the British abroad are less well behaved than they are at home: they are louder, ruder, less considerate. They not only insist on seeing and meeting English people everywhere; they also insist that the English abroad should not behave any differently from the way they behave in Birmingham or Twickenham.

In my own, old-fashioned way I still prefer travelling to tourism. I hate to admit it but I do not object to broadening my mind. The perpetual, unending excitement for me is people, ordinary people and extraordinary people, clever people and stupid people, pompous people and warm-hearted people. This being so, my great travelling hero is not Cook or Megellan or Francis Chichester but Livio Z., editor of an Italian newspaper, who never, never, leaves Rome.

"My mania is travelling, that's why I never go away."

This, I am ashamed to admit, was not quite clear to me so he had to explain.

"Travelling," he said, "means people to me. I want to meet people, first of all my friends. Now, if I go to London, you are likely to be in Tasmania, A. in Stockholm and B. perhaps in Rome. If I go to Paris—well, it is the same everywhere. But if I am staying quietly at home, everybody is sure to turn up in Rome sooner or later. This is the way I can see the world. Believe me, staying at home is the one and only intelligent way of travelling. It's more comfortable, less touristic and considerably cheaper."

He stopped for a second, then added, "Besides, staying at home broadens the mind."

". . . *we know you're in there.*"

The Night We Went to Epernay by Way of Tours-sur-Marne

Rolling English drunkard

ALAN COREN reports from Champagne

THIS is Fère-en-Tardenois. I'm damned glad I only have to write it down. I'd hate to have to try saying it. Not that I couldn't, all other things being, you know. I said it a lot this afternoon. I have a great French accent, sober.

I don't think I ever drank eight bottles of champagne in a day before, though.

Any minute the people in the room next door are going to start banging on the walls. You know the French; a volatile folk. Man starts typing at three in the morning, they can get very upset, pretty soon this room is going to be full of waving arms. I wonder if they have a hotel detective? What do you say to Rupert Davies at three in the morning?

I'd write longhand if I could, but the pen's in my jacket, and my wife is asleep on it, and when I tried to get my cigarette lighter out of the pocket a little while back, she went for me with her teeth.

Can you get rabies off people?

I rang down for room service a few minutes ago, I woke up, and the bathwater was freezing, and when I saw all the earwigs floating round me, I nearly had a heart attack. I couldn't move. I thought, there's enough earwigs there to eat an entire man, e.g. me, and then I thought, I won't show them I'm afraid, they smell fear, earwigs; so I started whistling, very slowly. And then I saw they weren't earwigs at all, they were shreds of tobacco, my cigarette must have come apart while I was asleep. I was certain when I saw a cork tip come past. I may be drunk, but there's no insect looks like a cork tip, that much I do know.

So I got out of the bath and I rang room service and asked for a bottle of Perrier, because while I was asleep someone had come in and carpeted my throat. Only—I could be wrong, but I think the Perrier is making me drunk again. I think it's getting together with all that dormant champagne, and I think they're cooking something up.

It's been a long day. I've had months that were shorter. It all started peacefully enough, we were coasting down Route Nationale 31, one of those undifferentiated cobbly ribbons rimmed with white cows that the French seem to go in for, and the next moment we turned south at Fismes, and there it all was. It isn't every day that you breast a slight rise to find an entire national character suddenly at your feet. On, as it were, the hoof. Slope after slope of little brown vine-frames, a billion budsworth of the '73 vintage awaiting its turn to be converted into christenings, wakes, seductions, ship-/

157

launchings, anniversaries, celebrations, commiserations, and just plain booze-ups. Thirty thousand acres of embryo burps, giggles, hangovers, and blokes walking into walls in the small hours.

It is this, the sheer *concentration* of Champagne, that first makes the imagination reel and grope: a mere thirty thousand acres to serve the world. Call for a bottle on the Ginza, snap your fingers in Park Lane, pop a cork in Valparaiso or Durban or Tunbridge Wells, and the stuff that pricks the nostril and galvanises the soul started off somewhere in these few kilometres, as a pip.

It would be hard to think of another patch of the globe's surface so rife with overtone, so alive to its own symbolism, and so much the quintessence of its host race. Here is the nub and concentrate of all things Gallic. As if there were a town called Tea, say, just off the M4, from which the whole essence of England emanated; as if there were Coke, Nebraska, or Guinness, Co. Cork.

We took the road to Hautvilliers, that sweet shrine above the Marne where Dom Perignon spent a large slice of the seventeenth century in glorifying God in an approved Benedicitine manner, i.e. by jumping up and down on the fruit of the vine until these products of the Almighty's grand design had been improved beyond all recognition, a heresy upon which successive Popes were prepared to turn a conveniently blind eye, especially in a good year. So we drank a morning bottle to old Dom, and the stuff fizzed in its two cones like liquescent gold, and the sun came out over the Marne. And we drove down to Epernay, across the river, singing, into the commercial heartland of Champagne, down streets called Moet and Perrier and Chandon, little alleys behind the high old walls of which the faithful clerks made out the lading-bills to Tokyo and Bonn and Manchester. And we dropped in at Les Berceaux and we had another bottle there, and that was even better than the first, and there were yet fewer clouds when we came out again; so we put the hood down, and we sang more loudly still, and we drove to Reims, because the good people of Heidsieck & Co. Monopole had asked us to lunch, and Reims is where they hang their hat.

Was it only a dozen hours ago?

And we drank three bottles of their finest cuvée, and we left them in the mild afternoon, and we said to one another How do you top that? but there was a spot we'd heard of called Le Château de Fère-en-Tardenois, and top it it did: a castle on a moated mountain, built in the thirteenth century and falling down ever since, due, claim its curators, merely to the ravages of time, but I have my doubts. I lay blame at the cuisine at its foot, at the Hostellerie du Château, where the food is so superb and the booze so prime, that when the last draught of marc has been sunk, one wanders out into the soft evening and up to the castle ruins, and, in one's euphoria, tends to bump into the hallowed reliquae with never a second thought. There's a sliver of crenellation in my shoe right now; the way things are, it may stay there for good, I am living history.

The dawn is doing things now. The birds are crazed. The sun is poised to warm the grape-buds out there beyond the ruins. There must be a hundred million bottles of the stuff in the immediate vicinity.

I may stay here forever. If I can find my other shoe.

"Do you wish to see Dr Livingstone privately or on the National Health?"

CAN YOU COPE IN A CROWD?

Do you find there are just too many people?
PUNCH answers some typical travellers' queries

Please recommend an effective crowd-repellent. I have tried rubbing myself all over with garlic, but it has little effect in Mediterranean lands.

Garlic is really intended for use against vampires. Many travellers nowadays prefer to coat themselves with rancid peanut butter. It is highly recommended for driving Scandinavian tourists out of catacombs.

A group of 200 American supermarket bosses, mostly called Chuck, recently pursued me by air all over Africa. Wherever I stopped, they arrived ten minutes later. On seeing me they would exclaim "Well, waddya know!", fall about laughing and insist on buying me drinks all evening. Is there any protection against this nuisance?

What nuisance?

I took my girl friend to the Coliseum in Rome in order to propose by moonlight, but in no time we were surrounded by jabbering young men. So many of them proposed to my girl friend that I could hardly get a word in edgeways. We tried again at the Acropolis in Athens, but the same thing happened. What do you suggest?

Try proposing in a box at the Coliseum in London.

It seems absolutely impossible to find a parking space in Rome. Have you any ideas?

Simply leave your car triple-parked outside any fashionable hotel. Try to live with congestion. Do not be for ever fighting it.

Is there any way I can prevent my bottom being pinched while standing with 200,000 people being blessed by the Pope?

No.

Is it possible for an Englishman to go through the souks of Morocco without being accompanied by scores of small boys crying "Charlie Chaplin"?

No. It is a custom of ancient origin which many English visitors find endearing. Remember that to an Arab boy you are indistinguishable from Charlie Chaplin.

I pride myself on being a reasonably fit woman, but in Pamplona recently I was hard put to survive a stampede of hysterical youths and maddened bulls. In the end I was able to batter my way through with my handbag. Do you not agree that Spain is becoming absurdly overcrowded?

Yes, but you seem to be coping splendidly.

Trying to escape from the pressure of tourists inside a well-known French cathedral, I took refuge in a cosy little wooden shelter with a seat. I was immediately badgered through a grille by an invisible figure who seemed to be asking what I had been up to lately. Is there nowhere one can be free from importunate humanity?

Why not sit down for half an hour in one of those do-it-yourself photo kiosks in railway stations? Just pull the curtain across and forget the world.

Can you suggest a way of getting a meal in a hotel dining-room which has just been invaded by a group, other than by a fat bribe to the head waiter?

Frankly, no. Face up to reality. Meanness will get you nowhere.

Seeking solitude in Finland, I was continually distracted by the sight of laughing naked girls leaping from lakeside saunas into he water. Surely one has a right to a bit of peace in the Arctic Circle?

Try Greenland. Much of it is still unspoiled by women.

My soul yearns for the limitless open spaces, far from the vileness of man, but I am informed that the only way I can traverse the Siberian steppes is crammed in a tiny train compartment for fourteen days with three total strangers, all speaking broken English and wearing rather awful pyjamas, with nothing to do but cut their toe-nails all day. Can you suggest anywhere else I can go?

See reply to previous letter. Or try Bognor.

Taking the advice of a friend, I leaned from the window of the boat train at Calais, and gibbered like a lunatic, in the hope that I could keep the compartment to myself as far as Paris. All that happened was that I was put under arrest for 24 hours, without food and water. My friend finds this highly amusing. Do you?

Not highly, just fairly.

Finding that people were in the habit of kicking sand over me and my girl friend on crowded beaches, I took a well-known body-building course and transformed myself from a puny weakling into a hulking lout, as a result of which my girl friend has just kicked sand into my face and left me. Have I any redress?

I fear not. You have come into this world at a critical period when the heightened struggle for survival has coincided with the general collapse of manners. Things will get worse before they get better.

While lying on my back on a bench in the Sistine Chapel, inspecting the ceiling through opera glasses, I was set upon by three women from some Scottish co-operative guild, who seemed to resent my presence beneath them. Although I repeatedly asked them to sit on someone else, they took no notice. Can anything be done about boorish behaviour of this kind?

See reply to previous letter.

All Quiet on the Aegean Front

Greek hoteliers are complaining of a desperate shortage of visitors, including LARRY

Oh Mr. Consul, What Shall I Do?

Before you become a Distressed British Subject,
read this warning by
E. S. TURNER

PERSONAL

Have you ever been a Distressed British Subject? Have you been thrown into a foreign gaol? If so, how did the British Consul treat you? Write in confidence to "DBS", BBC Television Centre, London.

NO, this advertisement has not appeared yet, but be sure it will. It is unthinkable that Distressed British Subjects, now being repatriated at the rate of over 3,000 a year, should not have a sympathetic programme of their own, like other luckless or wayward minorities.

What a studio confrontation it would make? On the left, a well-chosen mix of Glasgow Rangers fans, improvident adventurers, born losers and victims of foreign revolutions, each of whom has been sent home at some time with a non-negotiable travel ticket; in the centre, a panel of taxpayers who are convinced that their feckless compatriots should be left in foreign gaols, or forced to walk home; and on the right, a group of consuls, grateful for the opportunity to explain that, while they are men of exceptional compassion, they are essentially contact men and not travel agents, suppliers of motor parts, moneylenders, interpreters, arbitrators, employment officers, defence counsel, bail guarantors, lodging-house keepers, information bureaux or undertakers. Plus, of course, a wide-awake chairman alert to see that grievances ("You say that the consul told you to come back next day because they were holding a children's party?") are fully ventilated and official explanations are kept short.

Distressed British Subjects do not often crop up in the headlines. That shambles at Barcelona, when Glasgow Rangers supporters took on the Spanish police, resulted in the repatriation of 63 fans at an outlay by the British taxpayer of £1,558. The Barcelona Consulate consumed much energy and midnight oil before the mess was cleaned up. There are probably consuls who would rather have an earthquake in their territory than a soccer cup-tie.

Those 63 football fans amount to only one-tenth of the Britons who are helped home annually from Spain (the 1971 figures show over 600 repatriations from Spain, 950 from France). For the hippy kingdoms of Nepal and Afghanistan the figures are only half a dozen and two dozen; which suggests that many drop-outs really do drop out. However, the ease with which people can now reach faraway places inevitably increases the cost of sending home those who fall by the wayside. An "Australia or bust" expedition may well founder at Singapore, having already shed its weaker members anywhere from Calais onwards.

Consuls do not hand out tickets home lightly. Advancement in the service is not gained by becoming known as an easy touch for con-men. Anyone who requests the fare home is asked whether he has approached his bank, his relatives or his friends. While enquiries are being made he is expected to fend for himself. If his bank does not want to know and his relatives "decline responsibility", the consul endorses the applicant's passport so that it can be used only on the route home, issues him with a ticket he cannot sell and a small sum of sustenance money. The rules say that a person must be sent home by the cheapest route and it may be that air travel is the cheapest in the end. If a would-be Gauguin went to Tahiti and then got homesick, his repatriation route would probably be schooner to Suva then plane home; but he would have to tell a fairly heartrending story.

The distressed traveller signs an undertaking to repay the money. He is also informed that there is now a handling fee of £6. Back home, he may refund the advance willingly and even write to express appreciation for the help given him; or he may pay up grudgingly persuading himself that he signed under pressure, or that repatriation is taxpayer's right, or that a great nation ought to be proud to bring home its loyal subjects at its own expense from the corners of the world.

At present the rate of loaned money unrecovered averages about 14 per cent. MPs who demand to know what steps are being taken to recover outstanding moneys are liable to be told that many of those helped are in straitened circumstances and may be unable to repay for years, if ever. Instalments are accepted.

The notion that the Welfare State should defray the cost of foreign misadventures dies hard. Only a very few countries have reciprocal National Health arrangements with Britain. Hospitals in America and West Germany submit heart-stopping bills and it is no good handing these over to the consul; his disposable funds are earmarked for repatriation. Consuls are only too aware that holidaymakers will go to endless trouble to ensure that their cars are covered against all mishaps, but will take no such precautions on behalf of their families or themselves.

It is a somewhat shaming thing, that, even in days of mass travel, there are Britons who still cherish a resentment that foreigners are "not like us". They complain to the consul that a policeman "branished a revolver" at them. They object to being arrested for kissing in public, mocking flags and photographing railway stations. They find that those who flout the law are held in less esteem than in Britain.

It was for one class of lawbreaker abroad that the British Ambassador in Madrid, Sir John Russell, recently produced a warning poster which looks like something run off for Carnaby Street. The title, in the sort of vivid, jazzed-up type commonly called psychedelic, says: "The Game Is Not Worth The Candle". Both title and text would have shaken Lord Curzon. "This is an open letter to British visitors to Spain", the Ambassador begins. "It has just one thing to

say—stay off the hash". First offenders, he says, may expect six years and a day. "We have too many young people in gaol here already; please don't join them".

What can the consul do for his countrymen in gaol? He can see that they are made aware of what rights and privileges there are; that they are put in touch with English-speaking lawyers; that relatives are informed; that the gaol conditions are tolerable. Whether the consul can pay repeated visits depends on circumstances: the area he serves may be very large and he may not be allowed free movement. The Foreign Office advises travellers: "In those countries where travel is organised by the government the state travel agency may be better placed to help". So don't hesitate to try your friendly Intourist office in Khabarovsk.

Distressed British Subjects may be the victims, not of their own folly or improvidence, but of sheer bad luck in the shape of road accident, air disaster, robbery or revolution (there's a consul with some delicate problems right now in Burundi). Like the policeman on the beat, the consul has the cheerless job of informing next-of-kin, of comforting the bereaved. These are the times when he may grow a bit snappish if asked for his opinion on a disputed hotel bill.

In Angus Wilson's novel, *The Middle Age of Mrs. Eliot*, the British consul in a Middle East country takes the stricken Mrs. Eliot into his home when her husband is shot. She finds it difficult not to hate the consul and his wife for their kindness. That's the consul for you—the man you hate to love.

The rule-book leaves a good deal to the consul's discretion. As these lines are written the *Daily Telegraph* reports the discovery in Paris of two runaway boys from Leeds, found sleeping on the Seine embankment. After being put under Embassy protection these two distressed subjects "spent the day going to the top of the Eiffel Tower and seeing the Arc de Triomphe with Mrs. McCloud, wife of a British consul". If a consul is entitled to a seven-gun salute at his funeral, how many guns does his wife rate?

I'LL NEVER FORGET OLD WHASSISNAME

VINCENT MULCHRONE
unpacks some of his holiday friendships

A FRIEND of mine—old whassisname—once told me that a
man is lucky if he finds three real friends in the course of his
life. Very serious about it was old—well, it doesn't matter. I'll think
of it in a minute. A true friend, he said, was a chap who'd cut off his
right arm for you, who'd mortgage his house for you, that sort of
thing.

It put me down a bit, I remember, if only because I haven't got
the deeds of the property of any one-armed friends. I have a reasonable sprinkling of what you might call not so much dear friends as
near friends. If true friendship is Beaujolais, they are more Beaujolais
Villages. And, as more and more hair comes out trapped in the
comb, just like that chap in the ads for toupés, the more do I forget
their names. Like old, er . . .

It was June when I said to my wife, "I think I know who Joe and
and Mary are. The Joe and Mary on last year's Christmas card.
They're the couple we met the previous Christmas at the Brown's.
He was the big bloke on single malts and she danced a jig and
showed her . . . They were great. We swapped cards. We were going
to see a lot of each other, you remember. No, of course I can't
remember their *name*."

But then the festive season is a great time for almost making
friends, more especially since people began to travel. You can hardly
invite the neighbours in for Christmas morning drinkies without
including their visitors on leave from Singapore. He's a fascinating
guy, your wives click, and off you go again. By March, you're saying
"Charles and Sue *Who?*"

Had both sides kept to their tiddly promises, we might have gained
the divinity of real friendship, Aristotle's "single soul dwelling in
two bodies."

I sometimes wonder whether it's a punishment on me for making,
and forgetting, too many instant friends around the world. Along
with his passports (don't forget the extra one for Israel alone in
case some Arab immigration officer is feeling rough during Ramadan)
and the insect repellent, every foreign correspondent packs a meta-
phorical make-a-friend kit. When you land—and it's usually
because there's trouble—you are in dire need of a friend. Like now.
I have found myself evincing passionate concern for the health and
ridiculously low emoluments of a Levantine immigration officer, a
Bengali terrorist and even, on one ludicrous occasion, a Papuan
cannibal chief.

If you travel frequently on business, you'll scarcely need reminders
from me to tip *before*, to send flowers or chocolates to the hotel
telephone switchboard girls who can make or break your career,

"How far? About eight miles, but for you I make it five."

to pin an appropriate banknote to the back of your cable if you want
it to get away that night.

Where I fall down is keeping up with people who have the makings
of friends. Take Hymie. Or was it Schloime? Something like that.
When Jerusalem was divided he lived in the shadow of the dividing
wall and, owing to an unusual set of circumstances, gave up his bed
for me. He was a stonemason, but his army uniform was laid out
on his bedside chair. When the sirens went, he had just five minutes
to climb into it and run to the bus stop at the top of the street which
was his section's assembly point. He asked me not to leave my
cigarettes or loose change on his denim trousers in case they im-

peded him by so much as a second. In such a situation, you get to know people well. I did. I promised to keep in touch. I never did, though. It was Hymie. I think·

Then there was Indian Joe, Scout Commissioner of the Navaho tribe, who flew me all over the reservation in Arizona, an Indian patch about the size of the Low Countries. The Navaho have what they like to think is a rather British sense of humour, so for a Scout Commissioner they hired a Sioux and called him Indian Joe. In fact he's a Harvard man and wears Brooks Brothers' suits. So many Westerns are made there, said Indian Joe, that the Navaho have a set scale of charges, ranging from massacring a wagon train to just sitting on a pony on an outcrop and sneering at John Wayne. Charming man. His name will come to me soon.

And there was the chap who saved my sanity, if not my life, in Algiers, though all I can remember about him are his bloody cockroaches. Big as tortoises, they were. Step on one, and it would just snarl at you. They used to invade the kitchen of the hotel he kept rattling like a Zulu impi. I swear his chef fed them just to make them go away. I'd been thrown out of my own hotel, which wouldn't have mattered too much except that this was 2 a.m., Algiers was under curfew, the curfew was being imposed by the Foreign Legion, mainly Germans who, when they weren't singing the Horst Wessel, would spray a few rounds into the shadows. I was carrying a typewriter, two heavy bags, an even heavier hangover and had one of these patrols baying after me when Pierre, or was it Armand, opened the door of his cockroach farm and hauled me in. It was Africa's worst hotel. He was the world's nicest man. We became great buddies. I'll never forget old—oh, never mind.

The one I will always remember, if only because he had this foreign friendships thing bang to rights, is Joe Harsch, a great Anglophile who for many years was chief correspondent of NBC here. Just before his return to the USA I asked Joe to forget his Anglophilia for a moment and say what he most disliked about us. Reluctantly, he reminded me of the staggering hospitality most Americans offer visiting Britons. Over there "Come and stay for the week-end and meet the wife and kids" means just that. In a daze of booze and bonhomie, the English man says "If ever you're in London . . ."

Sure as hell he will be. He'll ring his old British buddy from Heathrow. "Hi there, Freddie, this is Hank. Just got in . . ." And what does good old Freddie say? He says, "Oh, er, hello Hank. How about a drink some time—say, a week next Wednesday . . . ?"

Now that I think of it, none of my foreign friends has been in touch for years. Hold on. You don't suppose they could have forgotten *me*?

The Sea and the Sky and the Bank Balance

We are always hearing about the ultra-rich, who throw vast parties in yachts like floating hotels, and about singlehanded round-the-world sailors; but what, R.G.G. PRICE wonders, about the singlehanded round-the-world millionaire?

Day 1. I managed to convince myself that having tugs take out the *Croesus* was within the terms of my bet with Lew. When they cast off, the automatic helmsman took over and we drove down Channel at high speed.

Landfall should be at a Portuguese resort where all the exiled monarchs have taken villas, away from all the Pretenders and Presidents on the run and exiled African rulers, who are not, frankly, out of the top drawer. You can't get anywhere to live unless your ancestors ruled before the French Revolution. I shall be expected to throw a party. Not easy on your own, but a challenge.

Day 3. Am I keeping the *Mouton Rothschild* properly? This is the first time for years and years that I have been more than a few yards from a butler or sommelier. How exactly do you prevent bottles from getting corked?

Day 4. Near disaster! A hundred guests and a hundred gossipwriters and I could find only one kind of caviare. Afterwards I was up nearly all night working on the ashtrays. What does one do with panties marked "Son Altesse Imperiale"?

Day 5. Quite a relief to turn out into the Atlantic. The waves look very high but don't seem to affect the yacht. Trying to get lipstick off necks of champagne bottles.

Day 10. Very lonely out here. Keep getting messages from William Hickey. Apparently my first's fourth is a Scotch Viscount. All my tinopeners but one have fused. If the last one goes, I shall be down to living on sides of smoked salmon from the cold store and lobsters from the chef's pond. How does one kill a lobster? Wring its neck?

Day 14. St. Vincent at last. The island is getting more trendy this month. When the news broke of my destination, plane loads flew in from Sardinia and the Shires and Hyderabad. HRH has announced that she will attend a fancy ball on board. Will my yachting cap and pyjamas be enough? Do I have to try to think of what I'm supposed to be? I'm going to have my work cut out shovelling all those flying-fish overboard. The prepacked buffet suppers have been got at by sea-snakes. How does one put pheasant breasts into aspic, starting from scratch?

Day 15. A terrible day. How I longed for the open, empty sea and just the sound of seabirds and blowing whales. Patrick Lichfield said he was not merely coming himself but bringing friends. To be on the safe side, I got out the second service but some of the gold had tarnished. If only I knew who the friends were, I should know whether they would mind eating off silver. What is holystoning decks? Lew radioed me not to overlook it.

Day 16. *Everybody* came to the party. The yacht was full of cameramen. One of the Greek shipping wives came with a pet armadillo and expected me to stop rushing round with ice and find it caterpillars. I am beginning to wonder whether there isn't a stowaway: the plovers' eggs are getting low considering that the voyage has only just started.

Day 28. A good run down the coast to Buenos Aires. I threw a gambling party for the South American aristocracy; but it is a strain acting croupier at three tables together. It was a relief to sail out to sea, heave to and settle down to clearing cigar stubs out of the baccarat shoes.

Day 29. I must say that, passing Cape Horn, I was glad the engines were so powerful. It struck me as rough. St. Elmo's fire attacked some of the aerials so that I couldn't get any stock market prices

until I was headed away from the Chile coast.

Day 38. I enjoyed the trip to Tahiti. I even began reading a book that the Burtons gave me, *Leaves from a Journal of Our Life in the Headlines*. There has been a good deal to do today getting ready for the people who are converging for my party. I find I can't understand the instructions on the churns of turtle soup. This could be important as they begin *Danger De Mort!*

Day 40. The party was a good one. But people do eat and drink fast. After all, if I'm opening the Napoleon brandy at top speed, I can't also be working the projector in the cinema, taking parties round the engine-room and cooking souffles at the tables. The stowaway turned out to be a Scandinavian professor trying to prove that the American Indians reached Malaysia by stowing away. If I don't get rid of him, I shall lose my bet.

Day 42.

Why can't professors take hints?

Day 47. Most of the people at my Singapore party were at my previous ones. That is the worst of air travel.

Day 55. Goa certainly has been discovered. We sat down fifty to lunch, of whom ten were photographers and busy at it. A Maharanee complained that I had not put pearls in the oysters. All she had to do was stretch out. I thought people wouldn't mind helping themselves if I dotted a few dishes of pearls about the table. Her husband owns some of the most fabulous treasure houses of the East. Palace life has made her lazy; but she was originally just school orthodontist at Harrow.

Day 59. It looks as though I'm heading into bad weather. The *Croesus* can give as good as she gets; but I was hoping to use the long stretch across to Africa and round up the west coast to work on the canapes. There always seem to be more parties in the Mediterranean than anywhere else.

Day 78. I was dusting the Giacometti this morning when I suddenly thought that, if it hadn't been for Africa over there on the starboard, I might not have been able to take this trip. Without my African holdings, I shouldn't have been much better off than my fellow directors.

Day 79. Sighted a lone rower. Thought it only decent to hail him and explain I should lose my bet if I had him on board. It was a girl. She said that anyway if she thumbed a lift she lost all her contracts. She warned me I was going to find myself in a shoal of sharks. It would need more than sharks to dent the yacht; but I could see she meant well so gave her a case of Imperial Tokay and some hams.

Day 82. Approaching civilisation i.e. Patrick Lichfield.

Day 84. Began my Mediterranean tour. Not quite sure whether this is de rigueur when circumnavigating the globe; but its a must for chaps like me.

DAY X. Don't know when it is. Don't know where I am. But I've made it home. At least the notices in the docks are in English. Phoned Lew. He says he wins the bet because I was supposed to go round to the east and not the west. Crew arrived back. They are polishing brass in rather a marked way.

"What I envy about them is the way they're here without all the trouble of getting here."

Where in the World Can You Love a Lover?

ALAN BRIEN suggests some locations where a company of two need not be limited

THE best place for a broad is abroad, as any professional bachelor will tell you, bringing out his little black book, full of first names and telephone numbers, supplied by his friendly neighbourhood branch of Interpoke. But where do you go, *together*?

What you need is somewhere which will mirror your fantasies. about each other. After all, you have the characters for your charade The dialogue can be ad-libbed as you go along. The plot is simple—boy gets girl—one act, in several scenes, with lots of intervals. All you are looking for is the correct back-drop.

It's not that the scenery at home is less beautiful. But when all around you is strange, new and unpeopled with memories, you stand out more clearly as a couple. The lover's illusion that only you two are really real is easier to sustain there. You want a place where the camera eye can identify you as the stars as it pans across the crowd. The rest are just walk-ons, bit players, spear-carriers and rhubarb-rhubarb mutterers. With an occasional eccentric comedy-cameo role as taxi-driver, head waiter, carpet seller, rickshawman or police officer written into the script for a character actor to show off his heart of gold as he beams at the handsome couple you make.

So first of all, it is often advisable for you to find a spot where you only speak enough of the language to find your way (and get your way) and where you never overhear conversations more interesting than your own and your dialogues are never overheard even in a crowd. Bad linguists carry our own privacy with us everywhere.

For noises off, and light under the door, I like water. Mountains and forests and grassy slopes are all very well on picture postcards—indeed they soon become picture postcards, only the colours are less bright, the sunsets less original and the clouds not so operatic. Water provides the essential movement out of the corner of your eye like a fire in a room. It is restless yet soothing. It gives you that cosy feeling that something is at work while you are doing nothing. And if it does spur you both to action, then it is likely to be the action you are after, the wish devoutly to be consummated.

The four settings for two that I recall most fondly are in France, Italy, the Lebanon and the Bahamas. The first, in Duclair, anyone can find in the *Michelin*. It has one rosette for food—but it should have three stars for its autumnal dinners on the wrought-iron terrace hanging out over a dark, lost garden, just four tables in the misted glow from the steamy kitchen window.

Serious lovers are always serious eaters—at least, mine are. And few things are more sexy than a pre-bed silence broken only by the heavy breathing and faint sighs of the diners, the clink of the bottles, the slurp of the glass, as the *pâté de canard* is slid aside after a third helping, and the fortifications of *moule* shells and *crevette* heads grow around each place setting.

And I would award a pink double-bed in any guide for those upstairs rooms where you sit next morning, propped against a pregnant pillow, warming your already warmed lap with a bowl of coffee-tinged milk and rustling-fresh *croissants*, while on the wall ahead, as on a giant home-movie screen, the window is filled with the image of the swiftly-sliding Seine and its noiseless traffic of cargo ships.

The second, in Venice, may seem more predictable but it comes far down in the Italian *Michelin* listing, amongst modest but acceptable *pensions* on the unfrequented side of the Grand Canal.

Ruskin lived here once and the food is appalling. But just round the corner is a *trattoria*, entered through a grotty bar, which opens out into one of those rare Venetian gardens, almost an orchard, where you sit under an awning of flowering trees, like Milton's Adam and Eve, while petals fall into your hair and *pasta* as a gentle, slow-motion snowstorm.

The bedroom has three windows, on two sides. At the foot, the vast, busy Giudecca, with its booming cruise liners. To the side, a narrow frothing waterway where beeping taxi-boats polish each other's paintwork as they just avoid collision at 25 m.p.h. It seems about as private and restful as a mattress perched below Eros in Piccadilly Circus. Until you close the shutters, laddered with sun-baked cracks, and the Venetian light, buffeted and bent by the sequin-scaled sea, projects on your ceiling a flickering, *camera-obscura*, panorama of the passing show.

The third place, Tyre in southern Lebanon, is on no-one's list (except perhaps pinned to the wall of an Israeli operations room)—a crumbling, cavernous hotel, its taps pouring rust into cracked wash basins, its lavatories overflowing, its bathrooms simply cells with perforated pipes, holes in the floor, like decontamination chambers. And its public rooms empty *salons* with cracked glass roofs bending over a few scattered rugs and collapsing divans. It most nearly resembled an abandoned Crusader fort, lately camped in by a raiding party of the Golden Horde. We were the only guests and met no other visitors to the warren except a naked wandering Nubian.

But it backed onto a more populous open-air restaurant, by the side of Tyre's shallow harbour where waves occasionally lapped across the floor almost, if never quite, dowsing the diners' toes. Great spreads of saffron-yellow rice-and-shellfish served by the light of candles guttering in the warm, spicy, night breeze. Strange fishes, with the lacy flapping wings of submarine butterflies, lined up to watch us. The wine was laboratory alcohol, faintly flavoured with sweet red grape juice.

But all night long, under our windows, which lipped the Mediterranean like the breakwater of a lighthouse, the sea pounded and chawed a few feet from our unsleeping heads.

Tyre may have changed since then. Four years ago, we had returned from a newly-shelled Arab village on the border, where coffins still lay in the streets, pools of dried blood were relief maps in the market, sobbing women in black threw dust on their heads. The road back was crisscrossed with barricades, manned by guerillas with

"It's the only way to see the country."

tommy guns and necklets of grenades. We passed lorry upon lorry of refugees, buried alive under furniture and chickens.

Death quickens sensuality. Loving couples seize upon places from which tourists have fled and inn-keepers open up for you alone, so long as you pay in advance, make your own bed, and demand no service. Something of the same feeling invests even seaside resorts out of season which also have that air of being deserted in advance of occupying troops, so conductive to instant intimacy and mutual dependence.

My fourth, the Bahamas, can provide that world-well-lost atmosphere at any time. Outside Nassau, where British exiles sit in their huge American cars, unable to drive more than 10 miles and 25 m.p.h. without falling off the edge, there are a thousand improbable islets. Each seems to be for sale in some part and you can be flown or sailed there, free, for a day of Crusoe seclusion with your hamper and bottles amid pantomime palms and sands.

But it is almost impossible to produce an exhaustive summary of bolt-holes for holidaying lovers. Often it is easier to be together in a modern hotel, even on the coach-tour circuit, especially if there is a Party conference or business convention, than in that forgotten backwater at the end of an unmade road where the locals eat strangers alive for a taste of company.

Remember the honeymoon couple who, when their friends cooed "Ooh, it's lovely in Paris," answered innocently—"Ooh, it's lovely anywhere." Even, I remember once, in the Strand Palace.

"*Everybody seems to be anti-American these days.*"

The Punch Italian Phrase Book

mussolini: a kind of small shellfish.

cellini: several small cellos.

risorgimento: a cheap peasant dish made from the leftovers of several risorgimentos.

colombo: a dove, hence a member of the Mafia who is anti-shooting.

cosi fan tutte: a kind of Neapolitan ice cream with five different colours.

Cognoscenti: a very ancient Roman family who own most of the props used in Kenneth Clark's "Civilization".

autostrada: racetrack.

Borgia: a top make of Italian racing car.

fellini: several small films.

perry como: a cheap kind of Italian wine made from pears.

basso profondo: after thirty, most Italian women develop a basso profondo.

il miglior fabbro: T. S. Eliot's favourite Italian proverb, which meant "It's better at Faber's".

e pericoloso sporgersi: a delicious Genoese speciality made from eggs, spinach and cuttlefish.

garibaldi: disparaging term for an ageing American film star.

Sotto Voce: Tony Bennet's real name.

Uomo Universale: highly successful Italian film company specialising in multilingual westerns.

andante cantabile: term applied to a slow but cheerful waiter.

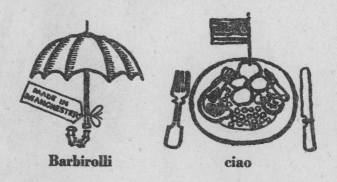

Barbirolli   **ciao**

oggi

pasta: basic commodity which can be shaped into different products such as stucco, fresco, baldacchino or terra cotta.

Gnocchi: the most famous of all Italian clowns.

Concerto Grosso: Tony Bennett's real name.

la donna e mobile: Italian garageman's phrase—literally, "the thing that connects the engine is working loose".

Sal Volatile: one of a number of legendary Italian art thieves (others include Ben Trovato, Al Fresco and Tony Bennett)

papa: derisive comment on the supposed celibacy of the Pope.

allegro ma non troppo: kind of Italian male who will pinch bottoms but go no further; also, basso continuo.

mario e franco: sundry items on a restaurant bill.

mazzini: small kind of tasty biscuit.

chianti: the art of guessing how much wine is left in the bottle behind the straw.

lamborghini: delicious kind of sparking-plug.

tempo giusto: weather forecast.

scampi: Italian journalists.

Tempo Rubato: Tony Bennett's real name.

con amore: service not included.

e pur si muove: "if it moves, pinch it".

antonioni: the state of not being able to grasp that a film has just finished.

commedia dell'arte: film festival.

tedeschi

pianissimo

AIRPORT

by GRAHAM

"The've called our flight, Margaret!"

BRITISH
PASSPORTS

"*Aha! . . . . what's this?*"

INFORMATI

"*Will there be much more delay? . . .
my husband's almost finished his
duty free Brandy!*"

*"We were well within the limit
on our bathroom scales!"*

"Where do we get frisked?"

"She said will passengers for somewhere I didn't catch go to gate number something or other."

"And how may I ask, does a ground staff strike in Las Palmas delay my flight to Manchester?"

Well, That's Hotelbiz

The story of BASIL BOOTHROYD'S historic trip across India

YOU'LL get no promotion this side of the ocean, they used to sing. The word has since been promoted into the public relations vocabulary, but the precept still stands. Anyway, comparatively. I suppose we didn't do too badly promoting ourselves into Europe with that well-known Fanfare, our only bit of recent native ballyhoo that comes readily to mind, and we were selling a whole country after all. But put it beside a routine American exercise the other week, selling the new Sheraton guest-tower in Bombay, and it sounds like a penny whistle played in a bag.

As Union Finance Minister Y. B. Chavan snipped the ribbon, his gold scissors hot to the touch, opening the tallest hotel in India, as if you hadn't guessed, and Chief Minister V. P. Naik cut the (tallest in India) cake, the band of the Indian navy let fly, champagne flowed like money, a blizzard of rose leaves showered down on name actors, princes, unfrocked maharajahs and U.S. Ambassador Daniel P. Moynihan, and one of the more sophisticated guests, from the international journalists' group, pronounced the whole thing quaintly old-fashioned. Hadn't shenanigans of this kind gone out with the Hollywood of yesteryear?

Well, I could be quaintly old-fashioned. I still think it takes a bit of organisation, from a publicity powerhouse in distant Boston, Mass., to turn out press and TV cameras at four in the morning—though this was a day or two later—to catch Joan Fontaine circling a lantern-hung, fountain-gushing lobby on a bicycle festooned with dabbawalla lunch-tins, applauded by harder-to-place faces from American television shows, Jumboed in from some ten thousand miles off: to equip the three hundred of us with invitations, movement orders, flower-decked rooms with complimentary Scotch and ballpoints and personalised letter paper (names in gold, what else?) to haul us, chairborne, to the top of Elephanta Island, boat us around the adjacent Arabian Sea, Boeing us down to Delhi, coach us into Utter Pradesh and the Taj Mahal: to puncture, somehow, the State of Maharashtra's Guest Control Act (assemblies limited to twenty-five persons) by an issue of plastic-cased Function Passes. . . . And we haven't even touched on the banqueting and band-booking yet, not to mention the scientific deployment of the air-conditioning to where it would do the most good.

Power was short. Stuck lifts wouldn't please. Water, too. It gave us an easement of conscience, as the fountains played, to watch Claude Feninger, President of the whole Sheraton shooting match, hand over a cheque for Rs. 1 lakh to the Chief Minister's Drought Relief Fund . . .

It was the Delhi departure that got us up at four in the morning. Some of us didn't like it. Got a bit grumbly. We'd been working hard since our eighteen-hour flight only three days before, confined to the aircraft at all stops in case we came back on board with hand grenades, and nothing to relieve the first-class luxury tedium but free food, drink and in-flight movies.

It had been three days of unremitting grind: receptions, luncheons, dinners, swimming-pool barbecues and rooftop suppers, balls, bands and belly-dancers . . . who can be particularly wearing if you've lived all your life in fear of being personally danced at, with a grave risk of getting dragged from your dinner table as an unrehearsed partner.

This actually happened to the impassively smiling Claude. It was after his second night without sleep, and he took it in his stride, shortly leaving for other promotions in Jakarta and Perth, bearing a commemorative plaque from Mayor Yorty, which itself must have taken some laying-on. Myself, when the jewelled navel came beaming in, I funked it, turning away to beg a cigarette from a nearby Prince of Nepal, who handed me a Lucky Strike and kindly prolonged the lighting of it until the danger was past.

So to be roused at that hour on a hot, dark morning, our suits, shirts and lingerie barely back in time from the laundry service and nothing to eat but breakfast—well. We'd hardly erased completely the honorary castemarks dabbed between our eyes on arrival. The floral garlands, draped about our necks on the same occasion, hung, still unwithered, on our abandoned shower fittings.

Rushed off thus on the long ride to the airport, sometimes crammed as many as five to a limousine, we felt a twinge of envy as our headlights picked out the peaceful rows of local residents, sleeping on the pavements, neatly head to toe, flanked by the occasional cow. No tours of New and Old Delhi lay ahead for them. They'd even be spared the second breakfast we were in for soon after touchdown.

There, amid the rolling parkland of a green, green farm, with fountains playing, and napery gleaming under coloured umbrellas, it would have been pleasant to nod quietly off, or dreamily contemplate our host's little son being trained over low show-jumps, and the film stars, ever energetic, being photographed on specially provided camels. But no. Tall, turbaned figures in deep gold belts

"If Lourdes is so marvellous, why do all the French girls have to go to London for their abortions?"

We were off on another three day's tough grind.

I think I stuck it out well. The unsuspected Raj in me. Mad dogs and Englishmen go out in 104°F. Some of the Americans felt they couldn't take it, and melted off privately to Kashmir, Katmandu, places like that. (I'd heard one of them enquiring anxiously about the Katmandu shopping potential.) As long as they got back to Delhi to use their return air tickets they'd be OK; though a few didn't want to return to where they'd come from, and fancied having their homeward flights stretched to other destinations. Tokyo, say. They had friends there. As everywhere.

"Do you know Paul?" I was asked by a lady whose husband, I had her word, had written twenty-nine books and was syndicated in four hundred newspapers. Getty, she had to explain. She tended to stay with him.

Somehow, at the last of the barbecues, after a six-day week that would have had Vic Feather in shock, I missed saying goodbye to my host and hostess. Perhaps they will accept this, the only intimation.

There wasn't a lot of light, that was the trouble. Just flickering flames under the phalanx of hot-plates, twinkling but purely decorative bulbs in the trees and tall hedges, the occasional flash-bulb, a few spots picking out the huge structures of ice-blocks. These had whirling electric fans beside them, the size of Spitfire propellers, until the heat of the night beat them, and they dripped, leaned and crashed, and were replaced.

Indeed, there was hardly enough light to enjoy the dancing bear, the monkey doing back somersaults through a hoop and not even knocking its hat off, the snake charmer with a small, alert shadow in attendance, which turned out to be a mongoose.

In the middle of it all, the word mysteriously spread, no formal announcement, that the cars were outside, and time was short to the midnight take-off home.

"Did you see the mongoose kill the snake?" someone asked on the way. "I was just starting to eat. There are times when you want to see a mongoose kill a snake, and times when you don't."

For most of the flight it seemed to be the middle of the night. Time trouble. The dawn kept ahead of us. I twice climbed the dark staircase to the Jumbo's penthouse drawing room, looking for someone else who couldn't sleep. The first time I found a lonely Trevor Howard, quietly genial in a sun hat with a striped band. He said it had been a good trip, and he couldn't think why he'd been invited.

The second, it was Jona Fontaine. She'd just finished a large crossword without actually writing in the solutions. She thought it had been a very good trip. Also that it was unrealistic of Nixon to recommend fish as a diet to beat the meat prices. Didn't he know that a pint of prawns cost eight dollars?

When it finally got light there was snow on the ground. Yugoslavia, I think that was. Waking for breakfast, someone read from a *Times of India* that the tallest hotel was expected to earn the equivalent of two crores of rupees annually in foreign exchange. We felt glad, I think, to have done our bit towards that.

Home is the Tourist

by DAVID MYERS

*"There, what did I tell you—
I just knew I hadn't left the gas on."*

"*I've a nasty feeling we've had burglars.*"

"*A little present for you—it's
got 'Palmas' running all the way through it.*"

"*I still can't get over that one of you in your bikini.*"

"*Don't you think you could remove that now?*"

"*He's naturally a trifle upset at your having deserted him for two weeks.*"

"*I see the Mortimers are back.*"